THE CHRISTIAN STUDENT'S

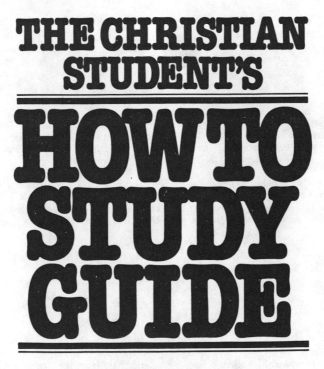

HOW TO STUDY GUIDE

JERRY WHITE

NAVPRESS
A MINISTRY OF THE NAVIGATORS
P.O. Box 6000, Colorado Springs, Colorado 80934

The Navigators is an international, evangelical Christian organization. Jesus Christ gave his followers the Great Commission to go and make disciples (Matthew 28:19). The aim of The Navigators is to help fulfill that commission by multiplying laborers for Christ in every nation.

NavPress is the publishing ministry of The Navigators. NavPress publications are tools to help Christians grow. Although publications alone cannot make disciples or change lives, they can help believers learn biblical discipleship, and apply what they learn to their lives and ministries.

Illustrations by Lee Schindler

Third printing, 1982

Unless otherwise identified, Scripture quotations are from the *New International Version*, © 1978 by the New York International Bible Society. Another version used is *The New Testament in Modern English, Revised Edition* by J. B. Phillips (PH), © 1958, 1962, 1972 by J. B. Phillips.

Printed in the United States of America

Contents

Illustrations

Author

JERRY WHITE is Pacific Regional Director in the United States for The Navigators. His 13½ years of active service in the Air Force included duty as a mission controller at Cape Kennedy during the most active phase of the U.S. space flight program. He resigned from active duty in 1973 and is now a lieutenant colonel in the U.S. Air Force Reserve.

He served as associate professor of astronautics at the United States Air Force Academy for six years, and co-authored a nationally recognized textbook on astro-dynamics. He holds a bachelor's degree in electrical engineering from the University of Washington, a master's degree in astronautics from the Air Force Institute of Technology, and a doctorate in astronautics from Purdue University.

He first came in contact with The Navigators as a student at the University of Washington. He maintained close contact throughout his military career, and helped begin Navigator ministries at the Air Force Academy in 1964, and at Purdue in 1966.

He has written *Honesty, Morality, and Conscience.* He and his wife, Mary, are the authors of *Your Job: Survival or Satisfaction*. They, along with their four children, live near Seattle, Washington.

Preface

NO ONE enjoys doing poorly or failing in a task. In college studies, doing poorly or failing will be obvious, since each term ends with a grade report which spells out how you did. And it can't be changed. It is part of your permanent record.

I find that most Christian students want to perform well in school. Many want to do well in school and also be deeply involved in a campus ministry. Yet the pressure of the moment and lack of knowledge of study techniques hinder them, leading to the guilt feelings associated with poor work and failure.

This book can change all that.

For the last fifteen years, I have practiced and counseled principles of how to study and how to integrate studies and a Christian ministry. I spent four years in graduate school, where these ideas were developed and tested. I spent six years as a faculty member at the United

States Air Force Academy and as an academic advisor, where I observed both Christian and non-Christian students succeed and fail. I still visit college campuses frequently and counsel students in the area of studies. Thus, this book is not just theory, but presents practically tried methods and principles.

On a visit to southern California, I was counseling a student when he asked, as he frantically took notes, "Why don't you write these ideas down to help others?" Frankly, even though I had written other books, the idea had not occurred to me. I prayed about it and asked others about the need. This book is the result. I trust that it will not only help you study more efficiently, but that it will also stimulate you in your personal walk with God.

Jerry White

1
Why Study?

DO THESE comments sound like something you have heard or said?

"Life is more than books and education. Most school courses relate little to what actually takes place in a job. Most companies train the employee for a particular job."

"All that counts is the piece of paper called the degree. After I graduate, no one will care what my grades were, so why bother now? I'll concentrate on what I think is important and let the studying go."

"Frankly, I don't know what I really want to do, so what's the purpose of knocking myself out on studies that are of questionable value to me?"

"As a Christian, I know that God put me in college to be a witness, so studies are low on my list of priorities. I need grades that are good enough to stay in school. Then I can concentrate on the important things."

"I'm studying engineering, so why should I bother with literature, history, or anything that doesn't relate directly to my major?"

Anyone who attends a university or college hears statements like these frequently. Perhaps you have had the same thoughts. And these statements are at least partially true. We can each point to someone or our own experience to validate some part of them.

Unfortunately, those who follow these platitudes play a risky game of chance with their habits, their future, and their inner character.

Brad Collins graduated from a small high school as valedictorian. He rarely studied, breezing by on his native intellect and the lack of competition in a smaller school. He was appointed to the United States Air Force Academy. By the middle of the first term, he found he was failing. He had never learned to study. Now he tried to learn under the pressure of the moment. He never made it and by Christmas had flunked out.

Chuck Turner squeaked by for three years in college, barely escaping academic failure by keeping above a C average by one hundredth of a point. He was rather happy-go-lucky about it, thinking that since he was a Christian and serving God, it would all work out. It didn't. He was dismissed from school in his fourth year. Most of his credits did not transfer (many schools will not accept C grades and below as transfers), and it took him almost three more years to graduate. After that he was only marginally qualified and work was difficult to find.

Robert Lundberg fumbled through high school fairly easily, never cracking a book, graduating more by putting in his time than by achievement. His high school diploma was meaningless since he learned very little. He joined the military partially out of desperation for work. There he became a Christian and began to study the Bible. It was a struggle since he lacked good reading habits, but he persisted and improved. When he left the military, he had new goals and decided to try a small branch of a major university. I shared several principles of discipline and study with him as he struggled through his first semester. He applied them diligently and did better and better in his courses. He actually received many A's, all the time remaining strongly involved in Christian activities.

I could continue to share incident after incident. You can see that skill and diligence in study, or a lack thereof, make all the difference in achieving success as a student.

Throughout this book I will use the term *college* or *university* for simplicity, but all the principles apply to any kind of schooling or training, including trade schools, apprenticeships, or specialized technical schools.

BASIC ASSUMPTIONS

Everything I share will be from a Christian perspective based on the Bible. Unless you have received Jesus Christ as your personal Savior, much of this will not make sense. This would be a good time to settle the question of your eternal future, before addressing your immediate future. If you have questions on this aspect of your life, see Appendix A for a further explanation.

You Are a Christian and Want to Please God

All that I write in this guide presupposes that you want to please God. However, the principles will work even for one who is a non-Christian. Often I will stress excellence and achievement, but only from the perspective of pleasing God, not pride and ego. "But seek first his kingdom and his righteousness; and all these things will be given to you as well" (Matthew 6:33). Our highest goal is to serve God. All other goals serve that supreme objective. Thus, fundamental obedience to God in the spiritual areas of your life is a prerequisite to success in study.

You Are in School by God's Will

You may wonder if it is God's will and take low grades as an indication that God wants you to drop out. That is a cop-out. Find God's will by direction, not necessity. While you are in school, you must assume that you are there by God's sovereign appointment. Thus, you need to do well. If you leave, it should be because you choose to do so, not because you must. Admittedly, you may be in a major for which you are not suited or in a school beyond your ability. If you fail, do not do so by lack of proper study techniques.

You Have the Basic Ability to Do the Work

We each vary in our mental ability. Only a few people are brilliant. Most of us are average. In the United States, most schools gear their course work for the average student. If you are accepted, by a school, it means some screening of your ability has occurred using various placement procedures such as the SAT (Scholastic Aptitude Test) or ACT (Academic College Testing). Your scores on these tests indicate your basic background and abilities. However, I have observed that most people succeed by hard work, not native ability, and you can, too.

You Do Want to Graduate

I must assume that you want to finish what you have begun. Without some element of this desire, life becomes existential—living only for the moment, caring little about the future or a goal.

A goal provides motivation. Paul was motivated by the call of God in his life: "Forgetting what is behind and straining toward what is ahead, I press on toward the goal" (Philippians 3:13-14). It is true that "a longing fulfilled is sweet to the soul" (Proverbs 13:19).

The Bible honors men and women who pursued goals. Many of these goals were not spiritual, but were still meant to glorify God. A major goal in school is to finish. A minimum goal would be to finish the term or the current courses.

REASONS TO STUDY

To Show Excellence

God uses common, ordinary people—in uncommon, extraordinary ways. The Bible describes many ordinary men and women who accomplished great things. They were people who fully used the ability God gave them. Excellence means doing well whatever you do. It separates the average Christian from one who leaves his or her mark on the world for God's kingdom.

God doesn't want "average" Christians. He wants Christians who characterize the excellence of Christ in their pursuits. Many people of Scripture were highly respected in their professions and communities. In fact, a requisite for leadership in the church is that "he must also have a good reputation with outsiders" (1 Timothy 3:7). It is difficult to imagine that one who does not do his work well would have much of a good reputation.

Paul was highly educated in the school of Gamaliel (Acts 22:3). He applied his learning both before and after becoming a Christian. He was a man who pursued what he did with all of his heart. In Colossians Paul wrote, "Whatever you do, work at it with all your heart, as working for the Lord, not for men" (Colossians 3:23). Paul's view of excellence invaded every area of his life.

Daniel and three other Jewish youths were taken captive to Babylon. There they were selected to receive training for the king's service because they showed aptitude for learning, were well informed, and were quick to understand (see Daniel 1:4). They were then educated according to Babylonian standards. Later the record states that "God gave knowledge and understanding of all kinds of literature and learning" (Daniel 1:17). Because God blessed them and they worked hard in study and preparation, they were chosen by the king for responsible positions. Daniel became governor of the province of Babylon. He was the epitome of Proverbs 22:29: "Do you see a man skilled in his work? He will serve before kings; he will not serve before obscure men."

The Bible contains many other examples of excellence. But note a word of warning. Excellence does not necessarily mean perfection. Excellence means that we do our best at any task and trust the results to God.

Your ability may not allow you to be perfect or highly skilled in many areas. But you can still work wholeheartedly at what you do.

Ecclesiastes 10:10 states, "If the ax is dull and its edge unsharpened, more strength is needed but skill will bring success. "A sharp ax requires less strength to cut wood. So diligent preparation makes studies much easier.

To Establish the Habit of Working Hard

Most successful people I know became so not because of luck and brilliance, but by hard work. "The sluggard craves and gets nothing, but the desires of the diligent are fully satisfied" (Proverbs 13:4).

The book of Proverbs hammers on the issues of excellence, hard work and wisdom. Idleness and laziness are condemned. Hard work is exalted and rewarded. Many students want to work hard—at what they like to do or what they think is important, but they miss the point. Working hard at only what we like is recreation. Working hard at an assigned task is the mark of a diligent person. In the world of work and career, most tasks are assigned, not chosen. The pattern of hard work which you set now will carry over into the rest of your life.

Most students in academic difficulty find themselves in that situation for one of two reasons; either they do not know how to study, or they do not work hard. I have rarely seen a student who could not do the work.

Just so you will not think this matter of God's view of work is simply my opinion, consider the following passages of Scripture.

> Diligent hands will rule, but laziness ends in slave labor (Proverbs 12:24).

> One who is slack in his work is brother to one who destroys (Proverbs 18:9).

> A sluggard does not plow in season; so at harvest time he looks but finds nothing (Proverbs 20:4).

Proverbs 28:19 gives the simplest advice. "He who works his land will have abundant food." Simply put, if you work hard you will do well. Hard work has no substitute.

To Fulfill Your Responsibility to Your Parents

Most students receive some financial help from parents in their schooling. Therefore they do bear some responsibility to their parents because of relationship and the financial involvement. In the Ten Commandments we read "Honor your father and your mother so that you may live long in the land the Lord your God is giving you" (Exodus 20:12).

Parents are not always right in their desire for their children to get more formal education. But in most cases they are concerned for your best interest. If they are supporting you at least partially, you must accept the responsibility to do well with their investment. Many parents make great personal sacrifices to provide for their children's education. As a son or daughter, you need to recognize and respond to this sacrifice in a way that honors them. Certainly one way is to study well.

When your parents do not provide financial assistance, the responsibility is not so clear. To determine your obligations to them in this case, do some study and meditation on what the word "honor" means in Exodus 20:12 and Ephesians 6:2. I think you will find that you still bear some responsibility to do your studies well because of your parents' expectations.

If college is not for you, don't take the easy way out by not working and flunking out. Do well at what you study and leave by reason of decision, not necessity.

To Establish a Profession

The end result of an education is not a piece of paper called a degree, but the establishment of a career. Basically you are building a platform for the future. For the rest of your life, you will be associated with your education and your work.

Granted, most students will alter their direction at least once after graduation or will enter a different career than the one for which they trained. Yet basic education forms the foundation on which other opportunities are built. You may wish to change fields by taking graduate study in a new or related career, only to find that your grades were too low to be admitted to graduate school. And you can't change them. I have occasionally heard people say, "The grades don't really matter. All that counts is getting a degree." That has a measure of truth. Companies do put considerable emphasis on *finishing* a degree, but they *do* look at grades, difficulty of curriculum, and specific accomplishments. They want a person who will work and produce. They can tell a great deal about you by your grades and your curriculum. Of course, the more specialized the field of study, the more important your courses and grades are.

To Have Greater Freedom

It has been my observation that the student who studies will discover far more freedom and opportunites, both now in school and later, than the one who does not study. When you know how to study and get decent grades, you free yourself from much pressure. Proper study all term long gives freedom as the term ends.

By gaining solid knowledge in prerequisite courses, the succeeding ones are made far easier. In one of my prerequisite undergraduate courses in my major I did very poorly. As a result I found myself under severe pressure because of lack of understanding of basic issues needed for the succeeding courses. I paid dearly for my low grade.

If you study well throughout undergraduate training, you inherit a far wider range of choices upon graduation. The mediocre student is fortunate just to find work. Learn to study well for greater freedom from pressure and increased opportunites.

PERSONAL MOTIVATION

Inner motivation coupled with personal direction from God builds the best foundation for achievement. The most satisfying motivations for studying or working hard in college are simple and straightforward. Here are some of them.

Obedience to God

The highest motivation is to please God. "Here is the conclusion of the matter: Fear God and keep his commandments, for this is the whole duty of man (Ecclesiastes 12:13). Jesus' question in Luke 6:46 was, "Why do you call me, 'Lord, Lord,' and do not do what I say?" Christ placed a great emphasis upon obedience and faithfulness.

Can lack of diligence in studies actually be sin? Yes, according to James 4:17. "Anyone, then, who knows the good he ought to do and doesn't do it, sins."

We must obey what we know.

Can a person ignore obedience in this area while reaping a blessing for obedience in others? It is questionable. Life is a complex mixture of full and partial obedience to God. Only he can choose what to bless in our life. But we do know that the blessing will not be complete if obedience in one area of life is consciously ignored.

Learning and Gaining Knowledge

As we probe the wonders of God's earthly creation, see his sovereign hand in history, or tap the creative genius he gave to people in such areas as art, literature and music, we sense the excitement of learning from God. For many people, learning new things motivates them to keep going. Many students find this thirst for knowledge lacking because they fail to grasp certain basics of a field of study. Then the struggle to survive academically keeps them from enjoying their education.

The primary purpose of education is to teach one to think, not so much to do. When we apply ourself and stretch the mind God gave us, we reap benefits in every area of life, including our personal spiritual walk and our future ministry to others. As we learn to think, analyze, and apply knowledge, we also learn to study God's word better, to relate to people more smoothly, and to develop our gifts.

A thirst for knowledge is a precious gift from God. Pray that you would receive it and use it.

The Future

We often put up with considerable discomfort, hard work, and even distasteful tasks for the sake of a better future. Many students do not truly enjoy school. But they go through the process to reach a particular goal.

Many plan and dream of great futures, but do not count the cost.

> Suppose one of you wants to build a tower. Will he not first sit down and estimate the cost to see if he has enough money to complete it? For if he lays the foundation and is not able to finish it, everyone who sees it will ridicule him, saying, "This fellow began to build and was not able to finish" (Luke 14:28-30).

The cost of reaching your goal for the future could be your schooling. Does the thought of your future motivate you to pay the price? It should.

Some argue that the future should not concern us. Doesn't Jesus say, "Therefore do not worry about tomorrow" (Matthew 6:34)? The only plans God disapproves of are those in which he has no part. According to Proverbs 16:9, "In his heart a man plans his course, but the Lord determines his steps." We plan and God leads us step by step. Ultimately all plans are a series of steps of faith that God will continue to lead and bless.

A goal, a plan, and God's step-by-step leading motivate us to work hard. At this point you may despair since you have no goal, and certainly no plan. I will discuss this in more detail later. For now, I encourage you simply to develop a general plan of study leading to a degree. You can always change your plans later. Someone succinctly said, "If you aim at nothing, you are sure to hit it." Aim at something.

IS STUDYING ALL THERE IS TO EDUCATION?

Perhaps you are thinking that I am overemphasizing the study side of education. You have a good point. There is a balance. Education should impart more than a skill. It should give a basic understanding of the world we live in and the ability to communicate to and relate to people. Education is much more than a degree. Other elements are social interaction, learning to think and discuss issues, and learning to appreciate our world.

The great scientist Albert Einstein put it well: "It is essential that the student acquire an understanding of and a lively feeling for values. He must acquire a vivid sense of the beautiful and of the morally good. Otherwise he—with his specialized knowledge more closely resembles a well-trained dog than a harmoniously developed person."[1] Study of academic subjects then, is only a part of education, although certainly a key part that must be accomplished to get the rest.

****

Life is more than books and education, but God has placed you now with books and education, so you need to know how to cope. When you develop the perspective that knowing how to study will *free* you rather than *consume* you, then student life will become meaningful and enjoyable. The gap between deciding to study and knowing how to study widens with each academic failure. But it need not if you carefully follow the rules of study outlined in this book.

NOTES

1. As quoted in *The International Encyclopedia of Thoughts* (Chicago: J.G. Ferguson Publishing Company, 1969), page 242.

2
General Principles of Studying

HOW MUCH MONEY would
you pay for an easy-to-follow, absolutely reliable method
for getting good grades in school? How much more would
you pay if the method required no significant work on
your part? The expression "There's no such thing as a free
lunch" applies here. So I cannot tell you that you will succeed in school with little or no work. But I can guarantee
that if you carefully follow the principles outlined in this

chapter, you will raise your grades signficantly as well as save time and energy.

I am so confident of the principles in this chapter that I can almost place them in the category of an easy-to-follow, absolutely reliable method. But the key is personal discipline and a willingness to follow the principles. You can pray, read books, plan, make promises, and get counsel. But without a measure of personal discipline, your effort is wasted.

Later in the book I will discuss further the topic of discipline. For now, I must simply warn you that no method of study will work if you won't work. I admit there are a few unusually brilliant individuals who seem to breeze through every course without study. I know a number of brilliant people who work hard. I also know some very brilliant people who did not study and got nowhere. Don't depend on your native genius or ability to do your work for you.

A FUNDAMENTAL COMMITMENT

After I received my bachelor's degree, I wanted no part of school again. I was tired of it. But in God's good plan, three years later I found myself heading back to school for a master's degree. Frankly, I was scared. I really did not consider myself much of a student, but I knew I could work hard. I also knew my tendency to get so busy that God could easily be closed out of my life. But by this time I had made a significant decision to honor Christ as Lord. I knew that returning to school was God's direction, so I made a fundamental commitment.

I covenanted with God to daily spend time reading the Scripture and praying before doing anything else at my own option. If I had a class in the morning, I planned to get up early enough to spend time with God first. If I didn't have a class, I would still have a quiet time before I began studying or doing anything else. Once I made this agreement with God, I never had to decide if I would spend time in the word and prayer. Regardless of the time of day, it came before study or anything else of my own choosing. It was one of the most significant decisions I ever made. At times it only involved ten or fifteen minutes, but I knew I was putting God first, and he honors that priority.

Whatever time you choose (and I strongly favor early morning), be consistent. Don't just "catch it on the run" in your spare moments. Set aside a particular time to meet with God.

This commitment to God lays the foundation on which the other principles are built. Any other priority makes the principles just another set of worldly maxims for getting ahead. They will still work in a functional sense. But you want more than something that simply works. You want God's blessing on your life and efforts. You want that measure of success only God can bring about.

Consider making this agreement with God:

For the next _____ months, I covenant with God to spend a minimum of _____ minutes daily reading the Bible and praying before studying or doing any other activities.

_____
(signed)

_____
(date)

For a biblical precedent for signing an agreement with God, consider Nehemiah 9:38. "In view of all this, we are making a binding agreement, putting it in writing, and our Levites and our priests are affixing their seals to it."

You will never regret making such a commitment. If you prefer your own statement, simply write it out according to your personal covenant with the Lord and sign it.

I would not want to deceive you. Work must accompany the application of the principles I will share in this chapter. If you try them, do so for at least one grading period. A few weeks proves nothing. The only positive proof can come from an entire quarter or semester.

PRINCIPLE #1
NEVER SKIP CLASS

Lectures and laboratories form the core of the learning process in our schools. No book can substitute for the personalized explanation by a professor or lecturer. Certainly, you can skip classes in many courses and later dig the material out of the text or notes, but it is a bad habit to begin for several reasons:

- Most courses do not follow the text precisely.
- Many texts need clarification through lecture or discussion.
- Some material tested on exams will be given only in the lecture.
- Emphasis on important material is generally given verbally.
- Hints and preparation for exams are sometimes given in class.
- Instructors may take attendance or know who is absent and take that into consideration on borderline grades.

I can already hear many arguments. "I can get more from the book than listening to him talk." "There are 300 in that lecture. I'll never be missed." "I have some of the worst lecturers on the face of the earth."

All of these statements contain some truth. Many professors do a poor job of teaching. Many course lectures are dull. And so on. But you will never lose by being in class. Before you argue against principle #1, try it for a term. Even with the worst teachers, you learn more by applying this principle.

When you miss a class for a legitimate reason, notify the instructor beforehand if possible and find out about assignments you would otherwise miss.

PRINCIPLE #2
NEVER GO TO CLASS UNPREPARED

Preparation before class is the key to understanding the lecture. Unfortunately many students simply take notes with little or no understanding. I have always tried to convince students that twenty minutes of reading prior to the lecture would save them one hour of study later as they attempt to put it together on their own. Preparation enhances efficiency in and out of the classroom. Many students get very little from the lecture because they did not prepare.

Again I can hear some arguments. "The comparison betweeen the textbook and the lecture doesn't exist." "I can't even get the homework done, much less prepare for the next lecture." "I understand the text better if I hear the lecture first." It is true that some classes are difficult to prepare for, but that is not true of most courses.

PRINCIPLE #3
TAKE GOOD NOTES

Unless a professor follows a textbook verbatim, you must take notes in class. The better you learn to take notes, the better you will do in that class. And the more you prepare for a lecture by reading, the easier notetaking will be since you will be basically familiar with the terminology and material.

In technical courses you need to copy almost everything written on the board plus helpful explanations. If you have read the text, you will recognize certain equations and can fill them in later, concentrating on the explanation. In liberal arts or social sciences, you will need to develop the ability to recognize and write down key ideas and phrases. Again, if you have read the material before class, you will easily discern which ideas occur in the lecture that were not found in the reading.

Every student usually encounters one very difficult course per term which requires almost as much work as all the others put together. Often it is a course which is difficult to understand. I have taken several such courses and so developed a survival system. After each class, I recopied my notes as soon as possible. I made certain I understood the logic or reasoning and added my own comments.

This process is time consuming and probably cannot be done for more than one course per term. But it proved highly effective every time I used the technique.

The books listed in Appendix B will give more detailed help in taking notes.

PRINCIPLE #4
ALLOT TIME REGULARLY FOR EACH COURSE

Most of us operate on the "squeaky-hinge" principle. The hinge that squeaks gets the oil. Or, in student terms, you put the effort where you sense the greatest pressure. Consequently, you find yourself behaving like a long-tailed cat in a room full of rocking chairs—frantically running from one place to another to keep from getting his tail crushed. You go from one crisis to another, never seeming to catch up.

Such a pressure cycle can be avoided by regularly working on each course. Many students study only to complete assigned homework or for a test. Even when work is not specifically assigned for the near future, you should regularly spend at least a few minutes on each course. This could be reading for the next lecture.

Especially in some liberal arts courses, it is possible to cram most of your work into a few days before a paper is due or you have an exam. However, this practice hinders a gradual learning process and tends to be a learn-and-forget mode of study. Some people excel at cramming, but most students experience only poor to moderate success.

PRINCIPLE #5
DO ALL ASSIGNED HOMEWORK

Homework generally falls into two categories; assigned but not collected, or assigned and collected to be graded. In my experience there is a high correlation between examination grades and homework preparation. Homework relates directly to the exam, especially in science or technical courses.

In liberal arts course work, the relationship still holds, but in a less direct way. Remember that the purpose of lectures and homework is to impart a skill or body of information.

The purpose of an exam is to selectively sample the knowledge or skill imparted. Few exams are comprehensive. Thus the point of your study is to understand the subject as well as pass the exam. You need to do both.

Completing assigned homework or reading cannot be

neglected without serious consequences. Certainly it requires time and effort.

But so does anything of value. If you wish to do well in a course, both are necessary.

You might ask, "Do you really mean *all* homework?" Yes. Most courses, especially undergraduate courses, are reasonable in the amount of homework required. However, there may be that rare course where the homework load is so great it cannot be done. I have never had one, but I suspect they exist. If you are astute in selecting which homework is key, you could do it selectively, provided the homework does not need to be turned in and graded.

PRINCIPLE #6
START PROJECTS AND PAPERS EARLY

Once I was assigned a computer project in an engineering course. Two students were to work together, so I teamed up with another Christian in the class. On a previous individual project, he had turned in his work quite late. I mentioned that if we worked together I had one requirement. We would begin the project the next day. He looked at me incredulously, knowing the due date was one month later.

We began the next day, and to his amazement, finished the project before anyone else in the class started it. We scheduled our work leisurely, used the last two weeks to casually make a run or two to confirm our results, and experienced no panic. My partner could not believe the difference from his previous project.

Whether it is homework, a term paper, or another project, the earlier you begin, the easier your work will be and generally the better your grade will be . Sometimes you lack sufficient information to go far very early. You may need later lecture material and actually waste some time by starting too early. But you can probably select a topic for a paper, make an outline, sketch out a research plan, and make a schedule.

Granted, a few students are geniuses at churning out quality papers in an all-night effort just before the deadline. But are you one of them? Why chance it, when you can do better with less stress?

Education teaches you to think. And thinking takes time. Beginning a project early provides time to think it over without the pressure of a deadline. The habit of leaving work until the last minute will hinder you significantly as you move into the working world. There the term doesn't end, giving a fresh start every few months. Your mistakes follow you for years.

PRINCIPLE #7
NEVER TURN IN PROJECTS OR HOMEWORK LATE

It takes no more time to do a project or homework on time than to do it late. Yet one of the common practices of many students is to turn work in late. Late work affects learning and grades far more than most realize. First, grades for late work are usually reduced if credit is allowed at all. Second, the value of the late homework is reduced since it does not coordinate with the lecture or class learning. Third, late work is generally done poorly in an effort to catch up.

Of course, we all know most late work does not result from a lack of time, but from procrastination. Whenever a reasonable problem occurs concerning work (such as illness), most professors will permit its submission without penalty if you make prior arrangements. Few are open to negotiations on or after the due date.

PRINCIPLE #8
DO AS MUCH OPTIONAL HOMEWORK AND READING AS YOU CAN

Most professors make suggestions for further reading or work. Often tests include some of the optional material to divide A students from B students. The more optional study you do, the better your results will be.

PRINCIPLE #9
ASK FOR HELP

Don't be afraid to go to instructors to ask for help. They generally keep office hours and will help if you do your part to prepare. If you really are lost in a particular course, don't wait until too late in the term to get help. You should develop a fairly good feel of your progress about one third of the way through the term. When you go to see a professor, write down your questions so you can phrase them well. Talking to your professor will give him an opportunity to see if there are other areas where you need help in the course. Be careful not to abuse your welcome, especially by not making an effort to solve the problem before asking for help.

If you cannot see your professor, talk with another student who you know does well in the subject. Many times another person can give you some help with your problem in a few minutes.

When homework assigned to me was not graded, I often found it helpful to compare or work with someone else. This is especially helpful on the more difficult courses. Studying with others for exams can also help in that preparation. But concentrate on study during your time together, not casual conversation.

PRINCIPLE #10
LEARN TO TAKE EXAMINATIONS

Have you ever known the material very well and simply blown the exam? Most of us relate to that experience. There is a science to taking tests. Some do it very well, while others seem to experience constant problems.

All exams are selective to some degree rather than comprehensive. *The How to Go to College Book*[1] has a very good section on examination techniques and preparation. I suggest you get it if you need help in this area.

Each type of exam, such as math or science problems, essay, or multiple choice, requires a slightly different technique. Here are a few hints you may find helpful. But remember, there is no substitute for thorough daily study.

1. *Listen carefully in class.* Most teachers teach their exams to some extent.

2. *Begin preparation early.* Don't wait until the night before the exam. If you begin short times of review three or four days ahead, you will find your mind continues to think about it even when you are not studying the material. Review your homework, since problems will likely be similar.

3. *Pray for help.* Ask God to give you insight to study the right things. As you begin the exam, pray that God will bring back to your mind what you have *already* studied. I never felt free to ask God to perform miracles of revealing answers to things I did not study. However, at times I had to recall material from a previous term and could not remember it. I prayed and found that God helped my recall process in an unusual way.

4. *Memorize important information, such as formulas, facts, or other data.* Check them by writing them down several times from memory. As soon as the exam

begins, quickly write out the information so you will not need to keep it on your mind.

5. *Read the entire exam.* Many students use time improperly in an examination because they don't know what the entire exam includes. Get an idea of what the total test covers. Choose the easier questions to answer first. Then tackle the more difficult ones. (This may not apply to lengthy multiple-choice tests).

6. *Read and understand the problem.* Many errors in exams result from failing to understand what the question is asking. It only takes an extra fifteen to thirty seconds to read the question a second time.

7. *Leave no question totally unanswered.* Do at least part of each problem if you can. Most instructors will give partial credit.

I recall one exam where I did not know how to solve *any* of the problems. I panicked, but then I prayed. I did as much as I could on each problem. To my amazement, I received partial credit on most of the problems and received one of the highest grades in the class.

8. *Recheck your work if you have time.* You may catch one or two foolish errors and increase your score by 5 to 10 percent. It's worth the effort.

PRINCIPLE #11
DO NOT CHEAT

You may wonder why I include this in a book for Christian students. Cheating has become a way of life for so many students that some try to justify it simply as the norm or on the basis of self-defense. Cheating violates God's commands for honesty (see Proverbs 20:17; Acts 5:1-11; Ephesians 4:25; Colossians 3:9), and it also breaks school laws.

The consequences of occasional or habitual cheating

are far reaching. It damages our conscience. It makes our degree a mockery. It mars our integrity. It establishes a habit of taking illegal shortcuts for the future. An entire chapter is devoted to this issue in my book, *Honesty, Morality and Conscience*.[2]

What about course files on homework and exams that are available in many fraternities and sororities? This is a difficult question. It certainly puts those who do not have access to them at a disadvantage. Some department and school libraries put exams on file and make them available to all to counter this practice. If you decide to use them, I suggest asking the instructor for approval. Many instructors are careful to use new exams, but a past exam can be very helpful in knowing the kinds of questions addressed in the course.

I do not recommend homework files because you too easily lose the benefit of thinking things through for yourself.

All in all, I urge caution on the use of files. Even when you are at an unfair disadvantage in competition with others, God can give you the ability and insight to succeed. You simply must study harder, and consequently you will learn more.

****

Well, there it is—your magic carpet to higher grades. You may say it looks more like a slave chamber than a magic carpet. Actually, there is no magic or mystery to doing well in school. It is simply a matter of discipline and work. Be sure you work at the right thing in the right way. These principles help you do just that.

These principles will work. They are not fanciful

theory. I practiced them repeatedly with good success. You may ask, "Did you practice them as an undergraduate?" Only partially. I wish I had known about them. They developed the way so many good things do—through bad experiences. I paid the penalty for their violation a number of times in my earlier years of study.

Can you violate these principles on occasion? Of course. Or you can adjust them to fit your particular style and needs. But make adjustments *after* a period of success in using them as stated.

The principles of study are general because they apply to any major or course. Each field of study requires a slightly different approach. Studying literature differs from studying mathematics. A history major would not be as solution- or problem-oriented as an engineering major. Appendix B contains a bibliography of study aids for various courses and majors. You can find help in how to grasp specific principles or teachings in a specified field of study.

You may get through school without following any of these suggestions and with less work. But why be mediocre when you can excel with a little additional effort and discipline? Try it for a term. I guarantee you will get results.

NOTES

1. Michael J. Gross, *The How to Go to College Book*, (Seattle, · Washington: Passage Publishing, 1978).
2 .Jerry White, *Honesty, Morality, & Conscience*, (NavPress, 1979).

3
Scheduling

BETH TURNER'S WEEK sped by in typical fashion. Sunday night found her cramming for a Monday test and writing a paper which was due last Friday. On Monday morning after the test, she had two hours to spare between classes, so she did a little shopping in the student union bookstore and drank a cup of coffee with a friend. Monday afternoon Beth did her laundry and talked with her friends until dinner. The evening was disrupted by a long phone call, a brief committee meeting, and several people who stopped by her room. She finally began studying at 9 P.M., but quit at 10:30 since no pressing assignments were due on Tuesday.

Beth slept through her first class on Tuesday but went to her ten o'clock class. She went to a noon Bible study and stayed to talk with a young Christian until her lab at two o'clock. After dinner she studied well.

Wednesday was much like Monday.

On Thursday Beth panicked, with a paper due Friday and quizzes in both of her difficult subjects. She studied two hours between classes and skipped lunch. Thursday evening Beth neglected to study her two courses since the paper took much longer to write than she expected. She finished at midnight.

On Friday she frantically reviewed between classes for the two quizzes. With a sense of relief, she took Friday evening off socially.

On Saturday she slept until noon and went to a football game in the afternoon. She managed to get in an hour of study before an evening group meeting.

Sunday was another cram day with studying after church and dinner. Beth had planned to spend some time that evening with some Christian friends, so again the midnight oil burned as she prepared for Monday.

It had been a busy week. Beth was discouraged because she felt she accomplished very little. And she had not yet started a term paper which was due in three weeks.

After reading the previous chapter, you can already see several things Beth could have done to prepare better for classes. How could she improve her week's schedule so that those last-minute panics and frustrations would disappear?

Next to knowing the principles of how to study,

knowing how to use time well is the most vital aspect of studying. This chapter will teach you how to plan your entire school experience, each term, each week, and each day.

STRATEGY FOR THE WEEK

A master study plan will probably crumble under its own weight in a week or two at best. Yet a plan for the week is strategic. Each week brings new demands and unique circumstances. Many students make out a weekly schedule (if for nothing else, to simply remember when to go to class). A month is too long and planning only for the day lacks perspective for the week. Thus your first priority for the term should be to make a basic weekly plan.

A Weekly Planning Page
As soon as you know your class schedule, make a master weekly planning page which includes mandatory and important activities. Include such things as devotional time, church, classes, labs, and your work schedule if you have a job. Figure 3-1 shows a sample blank schedule you may copy and use. Figure 3-2 is a sample of a basic schedule, those things that occur every week.

After including all the items on your basic schedule for a typical week, make enough copies on a copy machine to last you for the term (ten for a quarter or sixteen for a semester). You may want to begin with two or three copies to see if you drop or change courses and also to try the planning system.

At the beginning of each week (such as Sunday night or Monday morning), use a copy of your master schedule to mark in any additional activities for the coming week. Also include important study priorities if you know them.

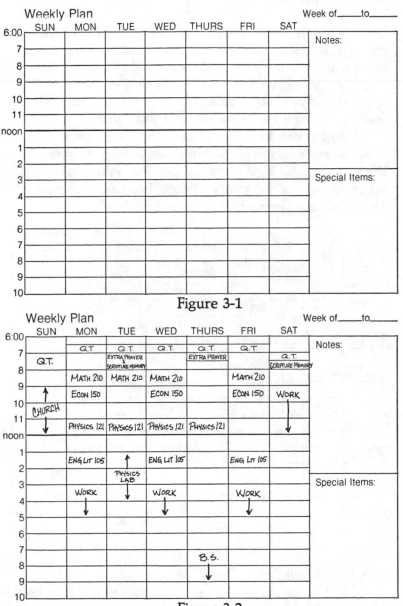

Figure 3-1

Figure 3-2

Your schedule for a particular week might include an exam, a committee meeting, a basketball game, an appointment with your advisor, and a class field trip.

You can include blocks of study time if you wish, but specific studying schedules will be planned daily. This weekly plan will be the guide for a daily plan.

I urge you to keep this plan simple. Some people lean towards more complex planning methods, but most find them a burden. Don't try to put everything on your schedule. If you do, you will soon become discouraged. Figure 3-3 is a sample of a filled-in schedule.

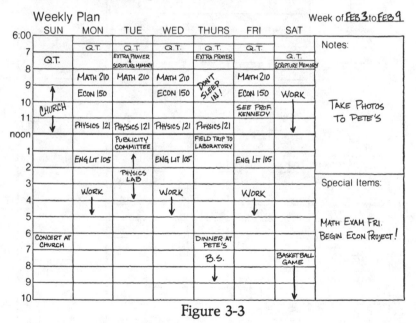

Figure 3-3

How Much Study Time?

Most of us study far less than we think. Days and hours slip by with much intended but little accomplished.

Even when we feel like we have studied hard, careful analysis reveals much less than we had thought. Time in study should not be measured by whether we "feel" we have done enough. Rather we must set some goals to guide us in time allocation.

I am convinced that most undergraduate students can do superbly with forty to fifty hours per week invested in class and study time. Thus, you can treat school almost like a job in terms of time invested. The old rule-of-thumb for study outside the class is two hours of study for every hour spent in lectures. Rarely does an undergraduate student spend that much time in every course or even reach that as an average. Certainly some courses require more than two hours and some considerably less. If we use the two-for-one rule, a seventeen-hour class load would require fifty-one hours per week total time, including classes.

Lab courses usually give one hour credit for two or three hours of laboratory time. Thus, the lab time includes the majority of the study time for that one credit hour. Often the required work can be done during the lab session itself. I recommend an *average* of 1½ hours of study per class hour (lecture). Some courses will require only one hour, while others will require two or more.

Consider two examples.

Case 1. Fifteen lecture hours with no labs. Time for study should be 22½ hours, for a total of 37½ hours.

Case 2. Fourteen lecture credits and two lab credits (six hours) equal twenty hours in class. Study time should be twenty-one hours for lecture plus two extra hours for labs, or twenty-three hours. Total class and study time equals forty-two hours.

Figure out your own required study time at the rate of 1½ hours of study per hour of lecture. Then make sure your schedule permits at least this amount of study time per week. Early in the term you may not be forced to study this much. But if you follow the principle of *regular* work for each course, you have accumulated study time for later when projects come due and exams are required. At least two weeks per term, you will probably need to increase your study time by 10 hours or more to accommodate tests and projects. Even that increase is bearable if you were scheduling 50 hours of work each week.

Suggestions for General Weekly Schedule

The more regularity you build into your schedule the better. Although you want to remain flexible to interact with roommates and friends, you need a commitment to planned times of study. Here are a few suggestions.

1. Schedule time for the basics of the Christian life on a regular basis: a quiet time, prayer, Scripture memory, and Bible study. Make them a priority in your schedule. You need to organize and plan your walk with God as well as your studies.

2. Concentrate on doing the majority of your work Monday through Friday.

3. Plan only part of Saturday as useful study time. When you plan more, it often gets disturbed.

4. Plan time off, such as Sunday. I found that I did well to plan for no study on Sunday. This was not from a religious "day-of-rest" viewpoint, but simply as a practical matter. The principle of a day of rest is valid. When you plan for Sunday study, you will probably leave more than can be done, and it hangs over your head all weekend. I found it to be a poor study day emotionally and physically. We do need times of spiritual and physical refreshment.

5. Plan for extra study time when you have examina-

tions, but don't totally neglect your other subjects.

6. Guard against impulsive scheduling, for instance, "Hey, Jack, let's go shoot a few baskets and get a Coke." It's great for interpersonal relationships, but disastrous to your studies. Do it occasionally, but not often. If you follow the outline in the next section, you may find some evenings free for relaxation.

7. Set aside time for laundry, shopping and other daily living responsibilities. But avoid using prime study time for these things.

8. Plan for adequate rest according to your need. Avoid staying up all night. If you begin depending on all-night or very-late-night study, you will ignore rational scheduling and do poor quality work. I suggest quitting by 11 P.M. every night no matter what remains undone. If you do this, it will force you to study earlier in the day or week.

STRATEGY FOR THE DAY

Your weekly schedule gives you a general idea of your day, but each day needs its own plan. The suggestions to you in this matter are so straightforward that you may tend to discard them for their simplicity.

Each evening or each morning take a three- by five-inch card to jot down a time plan that reflects the needs for the day. Figure 3-4 on the next page is an example. After a few days it will be much abbreviated, since you know your regularly scheduled activities. Then it might look like Figure 3-5.

The busier you are, the more tightly you must schedule. When you set an amount of time to work on a course, you do so according to an estimate of what you need to accomplish. Often you will not finish in the allotted time. I suggest stopping and going on to the next subject. Return to the one you did not finish later. Otherwise you tend to consume too much time on one subject.

Don't make a big deal out of this daily scheduling. It is designed to serve you, not to be your master. Even the few minutes before your first class starts is a good time. You might want to make a list of other things that you need to accomplish that day.

Hints for Scheduling
Most of us develop techniques and habits that save time. Over the years I have observed or practiced several things that will help many students in their studying. Try a few of these and adopt whatever helps you.

MON.

6:30	Q.T. (Quiet Time)
7:00	Breakfast
7:30	Scripture Memory
8-9	Math Class
9-10	Economics
10-11	Econ Homework
11-12	Physics Class
12-1:30	Lunch & Begin Math
1:30-2	Finish Econ
2:15-3:15	Engineering
3:30-4:30	Math HW
4:30-6	Physics HW
6	Dinner
7-8	Engineering HW
8	Open

Figure 3-4

MON.

7:30	Scripture Memory
10-11	Econ HW
12-1:30	Math HW
1:30-2:30	Econ HW
3:30-4:30	Math HW
4:30-6	Physics HW
7-8	Engineering HW
8	Open

Figure 3-5

Make good use of time between classes. The hour between classes frequently escapes us due to conversations or lack of planning. *Always* plan to use that time for some constructive purpose. You really don't deserve a break, do you? When you have a free period, go directly to a library or study area and begin work. The student union is usually one of the poorest places to go. Never go back to your room during the day unless absolutely necessary. Daytime study in your room is rarely effective.

Use Fridays well. The most universally wasted time for students is Friday afternoon between the end of classes and dinner. Most use it as time to relax. You must decide if that is the time to relax or if later in the weekend is better. I suggest studying hard during this time, as well as earlier during the day. You may find all your weekend work is done by Friday evening. Stay on campus if necessary to avoid the flurry of activity in your living area on Friday afternoon. Unless you schedule a Friday night activity, use that time for study also. Your goal is to free up the weekend as much as possible to be with people and for personal activities.

Use each weekday afternoon. Next to Friday, late afternoon is the most wasted time for students. What you do from 3 to 6 P.M. determines whether you study late that night or not. The more you do earlier in the day, the more free your evening will be for other activities.

Study in prime time. During study time, there are always a hundred other things to do, such as make a telephone call, do laundry, or write a letter. Resist the temptation to do routine things in prime study times.

Find a place to study. Not everyone can study well in the room where they live. In any group living situation, interruptions are the norm. Some people can maintain their concentration no matter how many interruptions occur.

However, if you find it difficult to concentrate where you live, find another place to study. The library works for some. Most departments in larger universities have libraries or study areas. If you use another place of study, try to use it regularly, not just when frustration due to interruptions overcomes you. Try it every night or just on selected evenings. Friday afternoon or evening is a good time to use another place because of the activity usually taking place in your house or dorm.

Learn the techniques of studying for particular subjects. Studying for a mechanical engineering course is not the same as studying for a history course. One who does well in mathematics may not do well in a psychology course using the same study techniques. The principles of Chapter 2 apply equally to all subjects, but the details of precisely how to study a specific course vary.

Studies can be divided into various categories:

- Liberal Arts (English, art, music, history, etc.)
  Such courses are characterized by demanding reading loads, term papers, and projects.
- Social Sciences (psychology, sociology, etc.)
  These courses are also characterized by time-consuming reading, research projects, and reliance on experimental theories.
- Business Sciences (accounting, management, economics, etc.)
  Business courses involve moderate reading, financial problems, computer usage, and projects.
- Pure Sciences (chemistry, biology, physics, mathematics, etc.)
  Science courses are characterized by problem solving, laboratory and research methodology, and moderate to heavy mathematics.
- Engineering (electrical, mechanical, civil,

aeronautical, etc.)

Engineering students take problem-oriented courses, some laboratories, mathematics, and computer usage.

Each of these areas require slightly different study methods.

- Liberal Arts

  Reading speed and retention, writing, and a good memory are important. Such courses require a grasp of broad concepts and the ability to express them.

- Social Sciences

  There is a great deal of reasoning and analysis, because there are few absolute facts and methods.

- Business Sciences

  Your study will require much attention to detail, as well as the broad concepts and methods of subjects such as economics and management.

- Pure Sciences

  There will be considerable hands-on detailed work, along with an analytical approach.

- Engineering

  Studies in engineering will center on application and problem solving.

From these descriptions you can see several types of courses and course requirements emerging which cut across several fields of study.

- reading for understanding and retention
- writing term papers or essay examinations
- theory with little numerical emphasis
- scientific theory
- practical problem solving

You will likely encounter two or three of these types of study in the majority of your classes. Develop appropriate techniques for each of them. Some will come easier to you than others as they mesh with your specific abilities. Study guides are available for most of these types of courses.

STRATEGY FOR THE TERM OR YEAR

Chuck entered college undecided on a major and unmotivated to study. Consequently he enrolled in general courses for the first term. In the second term he did the same. In his second year he was still undecided, so continued with a combination of general, less demanding courses. When Chuck finally settled on a major, he had few general courses left to take. He had to take full loads of difficult major subjects. As a result, his last two years were heavy with study in demanding courses. He was pressed for time and could invest little of it in Christian activities. In fact, he needed an extra year of study to finish his course work before graduating.

Many students find themselves unsure of their direction and major field of study. Christian students seem to be no exception. The tendency is to take easier or more general courses (which are often less demanding) to fill in the gap. Then students complete most of their optional course requirements and become overloaded with difficult and important courses later on.

Choose a Major Before too Long

Picking a profession at age eighteen or nineteen is not an easy task. However, you should initially make a choice between liberal arts and the sciences. Then by the end of the first year, select a major that could potentially satisfy you. You can change later. At least you will be headed in a definite direction and can begin taking required courses.

Spread Easy Courses Over the Years

Each term you need at least one course that you find enjoyable and easy. This will allow time for extra effort in some of the difficult courses. A term in which every course is in your major field of study makes college life miserable. But with a little planning, you can avoid this problem.

Be Cautious about Skipping Prerequisite Courses

Many schools allow students to skip basic courses and take the next more advanced courses. Be cautious about using high school courses as the basis of this decision (even with exemption tests). You can probably pass the advanced course with effort, but not easily. It may be better to take the foundational course and develop a thorough background in that subject. You may repeat material and experience some boredom, but that is better than getting low grades and beginning your college career badly.

I once enrolled in a course that my advisor thought I could handle. After one lecture I realized I was in over my head. I could have struggled through the course, but instead I immediately dropped it. I took it one year later when I had finished the proper prerequisites. The difference was like night and day. I clearly understood the material a year later.

Build a solid foundation, especially in your major field of study.

Don't Let Your Advisors Do All Your Planning

Many a student has reached graduation time only to find himself lacking one specific requirement. You are responsible to see that you have met all requirements. Plan your curriculum carefully. Check around until you clearly understand the specific requirements of your department or major. Begin counting credits at least two years prior to graduation. Don't rely on someone else to do your thinking for you. An academic advisor is just that—an advisor. If he does not handle your questions well, find another.

STRATEGY FOR THE SEMESTER OR QUARTER

At the beginning of each term, get a calendar showing the entire term. Write in the due dates for projects and examinations. You may not know them all at first, but record them as soon as you do. You may want to plan in such a way that vacations can be free of studying.

Also mark down any special activities such as weekend conferences or athletic events you plan to attend. Keep these in mind as you plan each week. Look ahead in your planning rather than look back as you get behind.

****

After reading this chapter, you may be saying, "That's too much regimentation. It will take all the fun out of college." It may be a bit awkward and unnatural at first, but it will pay great dividends if you try it faithfully for a term.

A university experience should be fun, not just studies. Using these study methods, you will have much more free time than you would have in any other way. Planning brings freedom, not restrictions. And the habits you develop now will last you for a lifetime and reward you many times over for the minor investment of effort expended now. Try it and then alter the suggestions if necessary, to suit your own personality and style.

Above all, keep a strong focus on your daily personal relationship to God. He is the ultimate priority of your life and the source of your success in school.

4
Balance of Studies and Christian Growth

TENSION between competing interests characterizes the lives of most people. Family, work, recreation, ministry, church, personal goals, and demands from other people vie for time and attention. Students feel many demands pressing for priority as well. Rarely does one have time for everything.

Handle tension between competing interests by finding the right balance so that the right goals are being met.

SHOULD YOU BE INVOLVED IN A MINISTRY?

The word *balance* generates a picture of a teeter-totter with people sitting on both ends. In your childhood, did anyone ever jump off the other end of the teeter-totter without warning you? It was a rude bump, wasn't it? Balance on a teeter-totter does not exist without a weight on *both* ends.

The very idea of balance implies at least two equal interests. Both are necessary for life to go on in a wholesome way.

Both study and a personal ministry (your total involvement in Christian activity) are necessary. We must simply deal with the creative tension between the two.

"My highest priority in life is my personal relationship to God and serving him daily."

When you work at a job, you still subscribe to that same priority, but you will devote more total time to your job than to your ministry.

Our logic attempts to force us to set mutually exclusive priorities; in other words, one priority overrides another in all situations at all times. But life does not work like that.

In reality we live with at least three or four top priorities, all of which *must* be done simultaneously. We must learn to fulfill the demands of more than one priority.

Granted, our first priority is to follow and serve God wherever we live and work. Beyond this, our priority while in school is to study and do well in our chosen courses. Studying is a student's job.

If you are a Christian, God brought you to school to serve him and to obtain training and help in your Christian life. But you could get that without enrolling in school. You could work at a job and meet its demands while serving God. But you *are* in school and it is God's will (remember the assumptions of Chapter 1). Therefore, one of your main priorities must be study. Your other major priority is ministry. You should not discard either one. But if one must go or be given less attention, it should be your ministry.

If school goes, your ministry will go as well. But note that reducing your ministry to some degree does not mean reducing your emphasis on a personal walk with God. School is your means for being in a place where you can grow and serve God now and in the future.

You *can* do both. Conflict between the two usually arises when you waste time or fail to discipline yourself in studies and thus create an emergency need for excessive study time.

Justification for a high priority on school can be found in Scripture.

> *Whatever* you do, work at it with all your heart, as working for the Lord, not for men, since you know that you will receive an inheritance from the Lord as a reward. *It is the Lord Christ you are serving* (Colossians 3:23-24).

Paul set the pace by working during his ministry.

> For you yourselves know how you ought to follow our example. We were not idle when we were with you, nor did we eat anyone's food without paying for it. On the contrary, we worked night and day, laboring and toiling so that we would not be a burden to any of you (2 Thessalonians 3:7-8).

It appears that Paul worked hard and still carried on his ministry. If God led you to school, then he expects you to work at it wholeheartedly.

Daniel set an example for us. As a captive in Babylon,

he was chosen for special training to enable him to serve a pagan king. His excellence at these studies served as an outstanding godly witness which is recorded in the Old Testament book of Daniel. Did he put God first? Yes. In fact, he put God's reputation on the line in a test (see Daniel 1:5-15). Did he work hard? Yes. Daniel did not attain his high position by laziness while being trained in the special Babylonian school.

If you were in a full-time secular job, you could not start your ministry until you had completed your required hours of work. No one is excused from work to have a longer quiet time, do Bible study, or witness. In fact, you arrange ministry activities around your job. In school, the flexibility you have in scheduling study and class attendance may deceive you into thinking they are optional. Remember, your full-time job right now is to be a student.

However, one who always says, "I have to study" and never finds time for Christian involvement errs in not fulfilling one of God's purposes in placing him in school; to grow in Christ and to serve others. Such a student simply *chooses* to invest time in other things such as sports, hobbies, dating, and clubs. The time is available, but it must be arranged properly. I have never met a student who truly did not have time for Christian involvement unless the student worked almost full time at another job.

I have rarely seen a true long-term conflict between studies and ministry. Some students who were failing have had to focus totally on studies for a period of time. But their problem necessitated emergency measures. If you follow the plan of a forty- to fifty-hour work week in school, plenty of time will remain for Christian activities. In fact, you will find that you will have more time than you ever realized *and* you will get better grades.

Develop the attitude that God put you in school *to*

study and to minister. Not one or the other, but *both*. Keeping that concept in mind will give you new motivation and purpose.

WHY SHOULD YOU BE INVOLVED IN A CAMPUS MINISTRY?

The term "campus ministry" means a particular group effort on a campus to reach out evangelistically to non-Christian students, and to train Christians in discipleship. The Navigators, Campus Crusade for Christ, Inter-Varsity Christian Fellowship, and several denominations as well as churches minister on many campuses in the United States and throughout the world. Frequently these groups assign men and women as full-time staff to develop an organized ministry to students. These are campus ministries.

You should be an integral part of a specific campus ministry. You gain much by involvement in a campus ministry. However, many Christian students try to "go it alone" or to form a private outreach.

Often students avoid involvement in a campus ministry because of the demands and pressures to grow and develop as a Christian. And some simply do not want that kind of pressure. Here are some advantages of involvement in a campus ministry.

Help for a New Christian
If you are a new or young Christian, you will need the influence and help of a group of other mature Christians to learn how to live and grow in your new life. A campus ministry can provide this environment.

Fellowship
Each of us needs fellowship to encourage us to keep

on track in the Christian life. When we don't have that contact, we find it easier to sin or avoid an outward witness to our faith. "Two are better than one, because they have a good return for their work: if one falls down, his friend can help him up. But pity the man who falls and has no one to help him up!" (Ecclesiastes 4:9-10). You need other people.

Personal Training and Development

Your student years mark the era of your greatest flexibility in learning. School is an ideal setting for your personal development. Spiritual training and development are crucial during student years. The habits, beliefs, and skills you develop in these years largely determine your lifetime direction and attitudes. As a committed member of a campus group, you will receive more personalized help and direction than at any other time in your life.

Mature Leadership and Planning

When I went to Purdue University, I found several Christian students who were related to The Navigators. They were trying to carry on a ministry, but there was no specific leader and little agreement on direction and activities. Since I was eight or nine years older than most of them and more experienced, they quickly banded together under my leadership. The ministry grew and developed significantly. I did little but supply mature leadership.

If all students tried to form their own small outreach, you can imagine the chaos which would ensue. By uniting with a campus group which is led by mature Christians, you reap the benefit of their experience and planning. You learn from them so you can lead at a later time.

The Campus Is a Mission Field

The attitude on a campus toward learning and experiencing new things makes it a fertile field for evangelism. One of your main purposes in attending classes is to interact with non-Christians and demonstrate the life of Christ. But how do you learn to do this? Campus ministries train students to witness and interact with fellow students. They form the basis of evangelistic outreach and exhibit a united Christian influence on the campus. The campus is your field for harvest. But it will yield little fruit unless you know how to sow, cultivate, and reap the spiritual harvest. Outreach in a group trains you for outreach as an individual.

Adult Transition to the Non-Christian World

This may be your first excursion into the non-Christian world as an adult. You can be strengthened for survival in the student jungle by more mature Christians.

Prepare for Your Contribution to the Local Church

Your future ministry and association will be with the local church. On campus you will learn many skills and grow spiritually in a unique student environment. What you learn now will lay the foundation for your ministry in a church as you graduate.

While you are in school, you should relate to a local church, though you may not be involved as fully as they would like. A good campus ministry will have good relationships with local churches and will encourage your attendance and involvement in one of them.

WHICH GROUP SHOULD YOU CHOOSE?

You may be on a campus that has more than one organized ministry represented. Affiliate with only one group. Don't try to fulfill the demands of two groups. Here are some suggestions on choosing a campus ministry.

1. Attend some activities to get a sense of what each group is like.
2. Don't make a decision just on the basis of other students' recommendations. Meet and talk with the person leading the group.
3. Be sure the ministry provides opportunity for small group Bible study.
4. Be sure the group has an evangelistic outreach.
5. Consider your personality and needs. Where would you contribute and benefit the most?
6. Decide where you will receive significant personal help and development.
7. Be sure the group is biblically and doctrinally sound. Ask other Christians about their reputation on campus.

Remember that no campus group is perfect (just as you are not perfect), and that it may not meet *all* your needs.

Also remember that in a group whose members are largely students, there could be a lack of maturity. Thus, you need to be more tolerant when plans, communications, and relationships do not always go according to your liking.

Get involved with a campus ministry. Don't isolate yourself and try to make it through on your own. You need the encouragement of other Christians who will help you develop your personal outreach on campus. They will also help you balance your life between ministry and studies, as well as give you spiritual counsel.

DESIGNING YOUR MINISTRY ACTIVITY LOAD

For a student with a normal credit load of fifteen to seventeen hours and moderate involvements on campus in non-Christian activities, what is a normal ministry activity load?

Two kinds of activity should be considered—regular weekly activities, and irregular events during the term. Consider these suggestions for a normal load for a student who does *not* carry a key leadership role:

Regular Activities
1. Participation in one weekly Bible study that requires one to two hours of preparation (three hours total time)
2. One weekly Bible study which you lead with younger Christians (two hours total time)
3. One weekly general meeting for the campus ministry, such as a seminar, rally, or planning meeting (three hours total time)
4. Person-to-person interaction such as evangelism or discipling (four hours total time)

A total of twelve hours a week is not excessive. Regular activities should not consume more than two evenings Monday through Thursday. Students with leadership positions in a ministry would invest more time than this. They have chosen this additional involvement and thus need extra discipline in their use of time.

Irregular Events
1. One weekend conference per term
2. Two one-half day training sessions or seminars per term
3. One major evangelistic thrust per term

This load would vary with the length of the term. Also note that one in a leadership role would have more demands. But the commitment level will also be greater and probably result in the elimination of some other extra-curricular activities. The sacrifice pays valuable dividends for the student, since leaders normally receive the most time and training from the campus ministry staff.

HOW TO HANDLE EXCESSIVE STUDY
OR MINISTRY DEMANDS

In spite of our efforts to properly balance studies and ministry, circumstances will develop where the study or ministry demands do become excessive. Let's look at how this happens and how to cope with it.

Consider excessive study demands first. Occasionally you get a professor who does give excessive work compared to the number of credit hours for the course. You must simply accept this as part of the school game. To be sure the work is actually excessive, keep an accurate record of your study time for one or two weeks. If you are investing more than fifty hours total time, your load may be excessive. (For some, the limit may be sixty hours.) Don't include a special project or paper in this time total if you delayed working on it. When class and study consumes too much time, you have only three choices:

1. Grit your teeth and finish the term, especially if you are halfway through the term and your grades in the course are good.
2. Drop one course. You may not want to drop the most time-consuming course since you would simply need to repeat the process another term.
3. Do less work and accept a lower grade. I generally do not recommend this unless the lower grade would be in one course only and would be at least a C.

The more advance information you have on the difficulty of courses and instructors, the better you can plan and avoid this problem.

When an excessive study load comes from your laziness or procrastination, your choices are the same. But you must learn not to allow this to happen again.

Excessive ministry demands can occur. Sometimes the demands are self-imposed by overcommitment, and sometimes they are imposed by the ministry activity load. This usually happens when there is student leadership rather than full-time staff leadership. In the section in this chapter on ministry activity load, you will find some guidelines on a proper ministry work load.

Evidences of excessive ministry pressure are:

- specifically scheduled activities four or more evenings a week
- demands for your time without personal discussion of your schoolwork load
- communication of an attitude that school really doesn't matter, but only ministry counts

One time I tried to pressure a student into attending a ministry activity. He declined coming because of studies. As I examined my motives, I found I was more concerned about the numbers at the meeting rather than his needs. I called and apologized for my pressure.

Sometimes, in our zealousness to help people grow spiritually, we push them too hard too fast. It is much better to allow them to select their activities with our counsel, not our command.

When excessive pressure comes from a campus ministry, you might respond in several ways. You could get angry and quit. You could give in to the demands and forgo your studies. You could sow seeds of discontent among others in the group. But none of these responses would meet biblical standards.

First pray and *make sure* that the demands really are excessive for *your* situation. They may not be so for everyone. Be careful to discern whether or not you are under pressure due to your own lack of planning or discipline. If that is not the cause of the problem, then see the leader of the campus ministry and ask for counsel, sharing your evaluation and dilemma. The leader may not realize that the demands are excessive. Frequently the timing of activities, such as near mid-terms or finals, puts the student in a bind. After discussing your situation with the campus ministry leader, make a plan to alter your ministry involvement for a brief period of time to see if that helps.

HOW TO RESOLVE CONFLICTS

Conflicts between studies and ministry will inevitably occur. No two cycles of activity can fit into a student's schedule without occasional conflict. Therefore, you will sometimes be faced with a decision. How can you know what to choose? Since you attend school primarily to study, should you always choose studies? Since you also must serve God, should you always choose ministry activities?

The key to this decision is prior planning. Most conflicts can be resolved by careful forethought.

1. Regular events like Bible studies should be put into your weekly schedule.

2. Anticipate when exams, papers, and projects will put pressure on Christian activities. Avoid conflict by following the suggestions of the previous two chapters concerning advance preparation.

3. When you find yourself in a time bind, give priority to the studies the first two times it occurs. But be sure to determine the reason for the problem

(poor planning, or an unavoidable conflict in scheduling) and resolve to correct it if necessary.

4. After the problem occurs a maximum of two times, give priority to the ministry activities and reap the consequences of not studying properly, if this was the cause of the conflict. This will get your attention rather quickly.

5. When planning for conferences or time-consuming activities, begin working at least two weeks in advance. With good planning, you need not feel pressured in your work.

6. Identify the most critical activities of the term and make a prior commitment to them. Do not give yourself the option of backing out. Too many students tend to view "optional" activities as expendable for catch-up time in studies.

7. Finally, remember that your basic source of guidance is from God, not men. Seek his will as you resolve the conflicts. God will give you peace when you choose his perfect will (see Colossians 3:15).

YOUR MAJOR VERSUS YOUR MINISTRY

Rick chose to pursue a difficult engineering major. He was a good student, but not brilliant. Consequently, his work load remained heavy. As a committed Christian, he was deeply involved as a leader in a campus ministry. In his junior year he decided to change his major. He chose one which required much less effort so that he could give more time to the ministry. The easier major was more general, not preparing him for any particular profession. He completed it easily, but found it difficult to get a job upon graduation.

Was changing majors a good decision? Sometimes

people in campus ministry staff positions may view the more difficult, time-consuming major as a hindrance to a student's spiritual growth. They may make suggestions like, "Just take a major that gives you more time to invest in people's lives. That's what counts for eternity." Who can argue with that statement? Certainly eternal values are more important than a secular academic education. But choosing an easy major may be a short-term gain for a long-term loss. The student fails to build a credible professional platform from which he or she will minister for the rest of his or her life.

When we consider world missions and the strategy of sending professionals to fill a job while ministering overseas, no one wants a poorly prepared generalist. They want experts—highly skilled, qualified, and able people. They do not want those who are unwilling to work hard and long for a worthwhile goal. In fact, we don't want that kind of person in full-time Christian ministry either, for he or she will transfer an easy-way-out attitude to things they do not consider important in Christian work.

A person who always avoids the hard tasks and seeks the easy way out never deepens his character or truly learns self-discipline and priorities. This person will likely spend a lifetime struggling to balance life and ministry.

Don't pass up a great opportunity to learn how to handle a heavy schedule while you also serve God. If all committed Christians took the easy way out, where would you find committed Christian medical doctors, political leaders, attorneys, scientists, linguists, business leaders and communicators? Yes, there is a cost to entering those professions. But if we believe that Christians should be salt and light in society (see Matthew 5:13-16) and serve as influential examples in the midst of a pagan world, then the cost is comparatively small.

It is true that among those God called to follow him, "not many...were wise by human standards" (1 Corinthians 1:16). On the other hand, God did call and use some extraordinary men. Paul was highly gifted and trained. Luke was a reputable physician. Moses, David, Daniel, and many others were gifted, trained men. God wants committed Christians at every level of society. As Christians we honor people who are already in positions of authority and respect, but sometimes we must be careful not to discourage those who aspire to train for such a life as dedicated professionals.

If God has given you some ability and capacity, use it for his honor and glory as a student. If you have the ability and capacity, you will not need to forgo ministry for studies.

So be cautious about pulling out of a hard field of study to gain time for ministry. Before quitting and taking a less demanding major, consider whether you have honestly applied the principles of Chapters 2 and 3. Be willing to work hard, learning how to discipline yourself now rather than having discipline forced upon you later. The student who cannot maintain a forty-hour study week as a single person and also participate fully in a campus ministry cannot expect to be effective later in life when he or she will probably have a full-time job, a family, and church responsibilities.

Keep a clear perspective on where you are heading over the long term. In so doing, there is no reason why you cannot receive the full measure of training and spiritual growth in the context of an active campus ministry.

Perhaps you are one who should recognize that not everyone should be in a tough, demanding major. If you must give your life to it with no opportunity for ministry, you probably are pursuing a profession that is not in line with your ability and capacity.

****

The balanced life does not come easily. But the best time to achieve balance is while you are a student. Grasp the unique, once-in-a-lifetime opportunity to develop the spiritual and personal patterns that will form the foundation for the rest of your life.

5
Self-Analysis

DURING YOUR EDUCATION, no one else causes you to fail or quit. You determine the outcome by the choices you make in the everyday affairs of being a student. If you know your strengths and weaknesses, you can be your own best friend. Paul succinctly stated the issue. "As your spiritual teacher I . . . give this advice to each one of you. Don't cherish exaggerated ideas of yourself or your importance, but try to have a sane estimate of your capabilities by the light of the faith that God has given to you all" (Romans 12:3 PH).

We need an accurate estimate of ourselves and the unique abilities God gave us. To know ourselves fully is a lifelong process. But in the area of studies the task simplifies considerably. Consider four basic areas:

- intellectual ability
- self-discipline
- past performance
- ability to assess present performance

Each of these areas is relatively easy to observe in yourself, but they require brutal honesty.

INTELLECTUAL ABILITY

Although it takes several years to develop a true perspective of your ability, you know enough now to help you assess your potential for success in college.

God created each of us with different physical and intellectual attributes. No two people are the same. Without question, some people are much smarter than others academically. You have undoubtedly met people who were obviously more intelligent than you and some who were less so. Yet intellectual ability does not make anyone superior—just different.

God must have had a great sense of humor when he gifted certain people intellectually. Many of them are totally ungifted in other important areas such as working skillfully with their hands, insight concerning people, and common sense.

I know I possess certain academic ability, but am often appalled at my lack of ability in many other areas. In certain manual skills, I am very clumsy, so I become very dependent on others to do what I cannot do.

We are intelligent in different areas. Some people are brilliant at analyzing an automobile or an electronic device. Others excel in academic pursuits. Intelligence and education must never be confused. Many uneducated people are brilliant, but simply were not privileged to have a formal education.

Since this book deals particularly with higher education, we will confine ourselves to analyzing intellectual ability only as it applies to academic pursuits. A basic intellectual ability is necessary to succeed in college. Intellectual ability manifests itself primarily as the ability to think, reason, analyze, and apply knowledge. Basic intelligence tests (IQ tests) give a vague indication of one's potential ability. They are not any guarantee of accomplishment. However, few people know their IQ rating, so it gives little guidance.

The best guide to your academic ability comes from standardized performance tests, past performance, comparing yourself with others, and estimates of your ability from others such as parents and teachers. None of these are conclusive by themselves, but only as they mesh together.

Look at your scores from the SAT's (Scholastic Aptitude Test) or the ACT's (American College Testing Program). The results depend largely on the quality of your high school education as well as your own ability. The percentile score tells you your standing in comparison to a cross section of students who took the exam.

For instance, a 75 percent score tells you that you scored higher than 75 percent of those who took it and 25 percent scored higher than you did. If you scored about 50 percent on either of these tests, you can succeed in college with considerable effort. A score above 70 percent more positively specifies your ability to do college work. A low score may not reflect your intelligence, but your *current* ability to do college-level work.

For your self-analysis, ask yourself the following questions:

Can I read well?

Do I enjoy reading?

Do I like to think and analyze?

Do I grasp logical explanations quickly?

Do I enjoy academically-oriented activities?

In high school did I do well when I worked hard?

A yes answer to most of these questions puts you at an academic advantage and suggests you should do satisfactorily in college.

SELF-DISCIPLINE

Your intelligence will be of little value without self-discipline. Many "average" people do superbly in school simply because they work hard.

Most of what I did academically came from hard work, not academic brilliance. I saw many people who possessed insights and abilities far beyond mine. I soon realized I simply needed to invest more labor to compete with them.

Without personal discipline and a commitment to working hard, you cannot expect to do well in school, unless you are in the 1 percent of students in the genius category who are naturally outstanding achievers in their college studies. For the other 99 percent of us, self-discipline and hard work are our lot in life if we wish to do well in college.

And, frankly, I feel sorry for those who miss the opportunity of struggling to succeed, for they miss the very experiences which develop character and a deep dependence on God. When success comes too easily, our appreciation for it fades. We take it for granted as though we deserve it.

Answer these questions to assess your self-discipline:

Do I finish what I start?

Do I avoid procrastinating in the less desirable tasks?

Do I function well without someone checking up on me?

Do I turn in work on time?

Do I keep working on hard tasks even when I would rather quit?

Do I exercise self-control over my personal desires?

Am I willing to work hard?

Do I generally meet my personal goals?

The more yes answers, the more self-disciplined you are. Remember, this evaluation is history. In the future, you can choose to be as disciplined as you wish. It pays great dividends.

"The lazy man does not roast his game, but the diligent man prizes his possession" (Proverbs 12:27). Proverbs teaches that one cannot be successful who is not also disciplined in mind and body.

PAST PERFORMANCE AND BACKGROUND

One of the best indicators of your future success in studies is your performance in the past, as well as your background.

Before taking this idea further, a word of caution must be given. When a person receives Christ and becomes a Christian, life takes on a totally new dimension. You are re-created (see 2 Corinthians 5:17). You won't suddenly become a genius, but your motivation and discipline may change radically. Your high school grades may not give any indication of your ability. You still live with the lack of learning due to not working in high school, but your ability could be far greater than your high school grades indicate. You may need to repeat some basic high school level courses (available at many junior or community colleges) to make up for your poor background. If you get the proper background, you could develop into a top student.

On the other hand, a good high school record is no guarantee of doing well in college. Depending on the high school you attended, you may have breezed by with little or no effort at all. Trying that in college leads to sure failure. Thus, standardized tests usually tell you more than high school grades. In general, the smaller the high school, the less competitive it is. The larger the school, the more significant higher grades would be.

For instance, in a graduating class of 200 or more, a grade point average of over 3.25 on a 4-point system would be quite good. In a graduating class between 100 and 200, a grade point average of above 3.5 would be very good. For classes below 100 students, no average can be specified since it is too dependent on the standards of the school and the specific competition. In general, one from a smaller school should have a higher average to assure doing well in college.

If you have already completed some college courses, you can use them as an indication of some of your abilities. Junior colleges and community colleges will generally be less demanding than a four-year college or university. Take this into account for self-assessment.

ABILITY TO ASSESS HOW YOU ARE DOING

Many students have a poor perception of their performance in a particular course or on a specific exam. Some are certain they got an A but it turns out to be a C. Others say they are certain they got a C or even worse. Then they find they got an A. Few students are able to predict accurately. Others remain uncertain, not venturing any guesses at all on their progress. You do need to develop some ability to determine how you are measuring up in a course, so you can make some improvements if necessary.

Can you identify yourself in this list of student types?

Joe the Eternal Optimist

Joe always looks on the bright side of things. Rarely does he realize he is doing poor work or failing. His estimate of how he is doing misses the mark by one or two letter grades. He shows very little discernment on exams, thinking he is well prepared when he isn't; thinking he did well when he didn't; expecting the professor to pass him even though his performance does not warrant it.

Martha the Eternal Pessimist

Martha always thinks she is teetering on the edge of disaster. To hear her tell it, you would think she should begin packing her bags to go home. She expects a C but gets an A or B. She thinks she failed an exam but does very well. Her countenance is always troubled or downcast.

Happy-Go-Lucky Stan

Stan gives the impression he really doesn't care about his grades. Sometimes he studies, sometimes he doesn't. He does well in some courses, poorly in others. Every grade report is a surprise. He carefully avoids knowing his course test averages or how they compare to the class average. If he knew, he might be forced to think about it and make some corrections. He would rather live in ignorance so that he can be carefree in attitude.

Hardworking Helen

Helen keeps working as though she were about to flunk out tomorrow. Even when she is assured of an A, she still frantically studies. She rarely has time for anything but study, for fear she will miss a possibility to improve her grades.

Accurate Art

Art may be pessimistic or optimistic, but he is usually right. He may be a good student or a mediocre student, but he knows where he stands. Before an exam, he knows how prepared he is. After the exam, he can almost guess his score. In general, he knows himself accurately.

As you try to identify yourself in the list, you probably find that you are a combination of at least two of these personalities. All of us would like to be Accurate Art, but few of us know ourselves that well. However, your personal experience should give you some idea of your ability to assess how you are doing.

Two major areas lend themselves to assessing your performance—individual examinations, and your general progress or standing in the course. I suggest that you keep a record of how you think you did on each exam and compare that to the actual results. From this record you will see your ability in self-analysis and also learn to realistically adjust your thinking.

Do the following in each course.

1. Understand the instructor's grading system.
2. Keep a record of your grades on the tests and any other graded work.
3. If the grades are numerical (rather than letter grades), keep a record of the class average, if it is given.
4. Frequently calculate your class standing.

Avoid optimistic thinking. Learn to know where you stand so you can make adjustments in your study time or emphasis. The facts may be harsh, but they force you to be realistic in your schoolwork. Self-assessment on exams allows you to analyze where you were deficient in preparation. Learn from your failures and make corrections.

****

The better you know yourself and your abilities, the more quickly you can adjust your course load, allot your study time, and increase your performance. Learn to be a student of yourself.

6
Should I Try for Straight A's?

SOME STUDENTS should attain high grades. Others would be wrong to try for straight A's simply because of the Herculean effort needed to get them.

Should a student get all C's? No. In our university system, a C average would indicate inadequate studying, except for a rare student who really was not qualified to be in college.

HOW IMPORTANT ARE GRADES?

Before discussing what grade level you should attempt, let's consider whether grades are meaningful or important. Opinions on this question vary from "worthless" to "of utmost importance." In some cases grades have been a true measure of learning. In other situations they bore little relationship to what was learned. Most students receive an unjust grade or two at some point in their college career. Grades present problems in terms of accuracy, fairness, consistency, and relationship to learning. They vary drastically with the instructor and type of course. But before we become too critical of grades, let's consider their purpose.

The basic purpose of grades is to measure the level of learning in a particular course. Of course, no system of grades measures learning with total accuracy. Any exam can only sample the subject and show if a student knows that particular segment of the course. Also, some students take exams and do well but do not possess a good understanding of the material. Thus, grades give only an indication of learning, not an assurance of learning.

But grades are important and do have meaning. Remember that course grades and degrees·are granted on the basis of a specified level of learning or achievement, not just mere attendance. For education and degrees to be meaningful, some system of measurement must be used. Grades are one such system. Comprehensive written exams are another. Oral examinations are also a possibility. But all these methods contain an element of subjectivity to determine passing or failing.

In spite of occasional inadequacy, grades reflect how much a student learned in a course. They form a permanent record of your achievement in school. For one who transfers to another school, they become very important for admission. Grades are also the key ingredient in admission to further schooling.

Some students mistakenly think that a prospective employer cares only about the degree, not the grades. Certainly the degree is key, but so are grades. In any competitive job market, an employer would consider the grade point average and specific grades as an indicator of a person's drive, ability, and learning level.

ATTITUDE TOWARD ACHIEVEMENT

A desire for good grades motivates some people to high achievement. Others care little for grades and focus only on passing the course. What makes the difference?

The difference is the individual's attitude toward academic achievement and ultimately toward success in any area of secular life. Excellence, not slothfulness, should characterize the Christian's life. Within the limits of our personal ability and capacity, God wants us to do well in our work and secular efforts.

Some students may consider it spiritual to sacrifice good grades for spiritual goals. Others may feel it is unspiritual to aim for success. Neither idea finds support in Scripture. Only when the motive for success centers around pride would sin enter in. In fact, Scripture supports the opposite view. Doing poorly has no merit when you could do well. As one friend, Bill Tell, stated, "It is never right to sacrifice your responsibilities." Keep in mind that doing well in this context depends on one's ability and occurs within a normal forty- to fifty-hour study/class week. An eighty-hour study marathon is not necessary.

There is no merit or reward for mediocrity. President Herbert Hoover commented appropriately: "In my opinion, we are in danger of developing a cult of the common man, which means a cult of mediocrity....Let us remember that the great human advances have not been brought about by mediocre men and women. They were brought about by distinctly uncommon people with vital sparks of leadership. Many great leaders were of humble origin, but that alone was not their greatness.

"It is a curious fact that when you get sick you want an uncommon doctor; if your car breaks down you want an uncommonly good mechanic; when we get into war we want an uncommon admiral and an uncommon general. I have never met a father and mother who did not want their children to grow up to be uncommon men and women. May it always be so. For the future of America rests not on mediocrity, but in the constant renewal of leadership in every phase of our national life."[1]

We do not want mediocrity. We want the best and we are proud and grateful when the best are Christians. But where will those "best" Christian professionals come from? They will come from men and women who grow spiritually as students *and* who do well as students.

Your attitude should be that you wish to do the best you can in concert with your ability and hard work, in the normal forty- to fifty-hour study week. Expect God to bless your efforts as you apply Joshua 1:8. "Do not let this book of the law depart from your mouth; meditate on it day and night, so that you may be careful to do everything written in it. Then you will be prosperous and successful."

This attitude and effort will build habits which will pay great dividends in your career later in life. In fact, the very habits and attitudes toward study developed in college will apply directly to quality Bible study and spiritual disciplines of life.

Success breeds success. Reaching your goals will encourage you in all areas of life. Learn to set goals for grades and succeed in reaching them. It will benefit your spiritual life and ministry.

Finally, our attitude toward the success we achieve should be thankfulness. When we succeed it is not because of ourselves. "Not that we are competent to claim anything for ourselves, but our competence comes from God" (2 Corinthians 3:5). "For who makes you different from anyone else? What do you have that you did not receive? And if you did receive it, why do you boast as though you did not?" (1 Corinthians 4:7). All our abilities come directly from God, and we are stewards of what he has given.

GOALS—WHAT GRADES SHOULD I GET?

From the previous section, you may get the idea that you must get straight A's or the highest grades your ability permits. No one works to the maximum limit of his or her ability all the time. We each waste time and fall short of maximum performance.

Are straight C's acceptable? No, not in a system where a C average marks the lower passing limit. If you set a goal of barely passing courses, you leave yourself no room for any mistakes or failure. You might set a goal of a C in a particular course if:

- The course relates very little to your educational needs.
- The course is very difficult and would consume an inordinate amount of time.
- The other courses during that term are so difficult and time consuming that something has to be neglected.
- Your overall grade point average is high enough to absorb a C without much damage to your record.

Only the second reason is truly legitimate.

As you set your personal grade goals, consider—

- your ability
- your desire
- your available time
- your overall goals

In general, most students should aim for a minimum of a B average (3.00 on a 4-point system). A 3.25 average is more comfortable and freeing. For an historically good student, a 3.25 to 3.75 average is reasonable. A few students will get above a 3.75 grade point average (GPA).

But how can you measure your own ability? We have already discussed several factors which will give you an indication:

- your high school grades
- results of standardized exams (ACT or SAT)
- college grades to this point in your education
- your ability and self-discipline

Use the chart on the next page to further analyze yourself. This will give you a general idea of your possible goals. For the ACT or SAT scores, use the following guide as an approximation. Please note that I have no statistical validity for these estimates. They reflect my personal interpretation of the meaning of the scores.

Percentile Score (Compared to College-bound Seniors)	Equivalent Grade
Above 90%	A
80 — 89%	B+ to A−
70 — 79%	B
60 — 69%	C+ to B−
50 — 59%	C
Below 50%	C−

In filling out the chart, if you do not have exact grades handy, make an estimate of high school and current GPA's. See Figure 6-2 for an example.

Remember several things when using this chart and setting your goals.

• If you were a non-Christian in high school and received low grades, you will probably do much better now.

• If your ACT/SAT scores were quite low, the cause may not be related to your natural ability. Perhaps low high school grades left you without the proper background for the test.

Lack of preparation for the test might have contributed. (Manuals are available to help you prepare for the test.)

	Overall	Math/Science	Liberal Arts (English, History, Language)
High school grades			
ACT or SAT scores (percentile compared to college-bound seniors			
College grades thus far			
Self-discipline level	✕		
Expected grade level			

Specific Goals.

1.

2.

3.

4.

5. Semester GPA goal

Figure 6-1

• The greatest variable in the chart is your self-discipline. As it increases, so will your grades and grade expectations.

• If your past performance is low, don't set goals which are mostly wishful thinking. Avoid extremes. On the other hand, when you have high potential, don't set too low a goal or you will not be challenged. As you work at setting and achieving grade goals you will learn to assess yourself and set reasonable, but challenging goals.

Many schools now offer students the option of taking a course in which they either pass or fail, rather than receive a letter grade. Should a student take this option? Rarely. Pass/fail measures only minimum achievement. A prospective employer looking at a record with frequent P/F courses would immediately know the student was tak-

	Overall	Math/Science	Liberal Arts (English, History, Language)
High school grades	3.12	2.8	3.3
ACT or SAT scores (percentile compared to college-bound seniors	81 (B+)	78 (B)	91 (A)
College grades thus far	2.8	2.4	3.0
Self-discipline level		MEDIUM	MED-HIGH
Expected grade level	B+	B	A

Specific Goals.

1. ENGLISH 210   A
2. HISTORY 150   A- OR B+
3. MATH 112   B
4. PSYCH 201   A
5. Semester GPA goal 3.4

Figure 6-2

ing the easy way out.

The one exception to this would be P/F courses in a highly respected school where failure would be equivalent to any grade below a B. Whenever possible, take the course for a letter grade. However, an occasional P/F course in a non—major subject certainly would be acceptable.

HOW GOOD GRADES WILL BENEFIT YOU

Several key benefits result from achieving good grades. Let's consider some of these benefits.

1. The greatest benefit is the *freedom* you achieve by not being under too much pressure to produce in later school years. You can then afford a lower grade or two if hard courses and ministry pressures increase.

2. Good grades pave the way to attend *graduate school*. Generally, a minimum GPA of 3.0 is required for most graduate schools. The other entrance requirement is the Graduate Record Examination (GRE) which can offset the effect of lower grades. Undergraduate students often do not expect to go to graduate school, but later see the need. Whether graduate school is a goal or not, a minimum of 3.0 GPA leaves that door open.

3. Good grades will help you in your *employment and career*. Though grades are only part of what a prospective employer looks at, they do result in a judgment on your drive, ability and achievement.

4. Many serious Christian students want to serve God overseas by working in their profession. What they do not realize is that *overseas employment* requires specialized skills, proven performance, and high achievement. For overseas positions, companies simply do not invest in employees who are marginally qualified. Foreign govern-

ments hire only unusually qualified or skilled people from another country to fill their jobs.

5. Good grades give you a *good testimony* and a *sense of achievement.* As you do well, you build a platform on which to demonstrate God's blessing in your life. You also develop confidence which results in further achievement.

It is wise for leaders of campus ministries to set a minimum grade requirement for those students who are in leadership positions. Low grades should disqualify students from active leadership in a campus ministry, just as a poor work reputation would disqualify one from being an elder in a church (see 1 Timothy 3:7 and 2 Thessalonians 3:6-12). Poor students soon fail to exercise any leadership at all.

****

Should you get straight A's? Yes, if they are within reach. The important thing is to do as well as you can within the limits of your ability and personal goals.

NOTES

1. As quoted in *Bits and Pieces,* (Fairfield, New Jersey: Economics Press, February, 1977), pages 20-21.

7
Major Problems

ACADEMIC PROBLEMS will
not be solved without significant effort on your part. You
can pray, keep a good spiritual walk with God, and
witness regularly, but without hard work you will still fail.
Some wise saint commented, "Pray as though it all
depended on God and work as though it all depended on
you." The theology of that statement may be debatable,
but certainly its practical truth communicates that we need

both dependence on God and hard work.

This chapter discusses some problems which many students grapple with at some point in their college career.

PROCRASTINATION AND LAZINESS

> I count him braver who overcomes his desire, than him who conquers his enemies, for the hardest victory is the victory over self.[1]
>
> —Aristotle

The only way to overcome procrastination or laziness is to change your habits. You must exert self-discipline. The principles of Chapter 2 give you specifics on what you need to do, but *you* must do it. All the gimmicks and study hints are useless unless you apply them.

You must develop personal self-discipline for success in any area of life. God has given you the ability for self-discipline and only needs your cooperation. The French author Victor Hugo said, "People do not lack strength; they lack will."[2] We need to exercise our will to do God's will.

But how does one acquire self-discipline? The first step is to desire a goal that self-discipline will help you reach. The second step is to make a plan or schedule and commit yourself before God to keep it. Have a friend check up on you. The third step is to begin a steady process of destroying bad habits and developing new ones. Finally, you must keep this pressure on yourself long enough to actually experience some of its benefits and to see your goal realized.

CATCHING UP

Everyone gets behind at some time or another. How can

you catch up? If you are far behind in a course (over two weeks), you may need to drop it. When you are moderately behind, you have several alternatives:

1. Don't catch up and take a lower grade.
2. Catch up bit by bit over several weeks.
3. Catch up by total concentration on that subject for a period of a few days.
4. Drop the course.

Let's assume that you wish to catch up by pursuing the second or third options. Follow this process:

1. Separate the work that is not done into that which can be (or must be) turned in for grade and that which is necessary for learning.
2. Cancel those activities which are not mandatory for the next few days.
3. Plan on some time of total concentration (for example, all day Saturday).
4. Check ahead of time to be sure you have the material you need to complete the work in the course.
5. Do the most recently assigned work first to turn in for maximum grade. Don't neglect currently due assignments to do late work.
6. Do required late work which must be turned in.
7. Do back work for understanding and exam preparation.

Above all, talk to your professors. Let them know you are working on catching up. If you have a legitimate problem, they can be very understanding, and may even agree to extend deadlines. Make yourself known and work with the instructor. A little communication makes a great difference.

Recently both my son and daughter were behind in different courses. I encouraged them to talk to the instructor. One had an exam delayed and the other had a lab report deadline delayed. The student who never talks to the instructor and silently flunks gets very little understanding from a professor.

Obviously, you cannot apply this catch-up process frequently. Also, do not cancel ministry activities to catch up without giving it some thought and prayer.

If you habitually fall behind, you may need to reap the results and take lower grades. You cannot always operate in a panic, neglecting ministry and other important activities.

The major problem of a heavy catch-up effort comes when other current courses suffer. Discipline yourself to keep up in your work.

LOSING MOTIVATION

Many students lose their motivation to study for many reasons:

- physical illness
- emotional stress
- sin
- dislike for a subject
- lack of goals
- doubting their life direction
- questioning their current major
- doing poorly in school

You can discern between losing motivation and laziness by comparing your situation now with that earlier in the term or year. If you were doing well weeks or months before and now lack incentive to study, this would be loss of motivation. If your present situation resembles how you constantly function, it is a problem of laziness.

How can you rekindle your motivation?

1. Keep working as an act of your will. Often perseverance carries you through such a period.
2. Examine yourself spiritually to see if there is an area of sin or a spiritual problem in your life. If so, take it to God.
3. Guard your physical fitness, nutrition, and rest.
4. Attempt to identify the specific reasons for your loss of motivation. You may need to reevaluate your goals or your major field of study.
5. Seek counsel with a mature Christian friend to help discern your need and to set up a plan for correcting it.
6. Ask God to give you the proper inner motivation to work with the right motives and purpose.
7. Spend extra time in the word and prayer, for true motivation comes from God. "My flesh and my heart may fail, but God is the strength of my heart and my portion forever" (Psalm 73:26). A person's motivation can be revived, but it takes time to do so. Learn to discipline yourself to keep going, and to wait on God to rekindle the motivation.

OVERCOMING A POOR
ACADEMIC BACKGROUND

Some students do poor work, not because of lack of ability, but because they possess an inadequate academic background. Several things may have contributed to poor academic preparation, such as:
- attending a poor high school
- attending a small high school where competition was low and a student could survive on native ability rather than hard work
- a history of poor study habits

- taking easy courses, thus neglecting the necessary background for college
- several years between high school and college, during which time much material is forgotten
- weakness in a particular area of study, perhaps math or English

Regardless of the reason, you must do something about it. Don't take courses for which you are not prepared. You may flunk. Get the proper background by doing the following:

1. Identify the specific area of need.
2. If necessary, take some tests to help you discern your need. School counselors will direct you.
3. Review or take high school level courses to bring your background to an acceptable level. You can often do this in college for no credit or at a community college. Even if it takes you a year, obtain the proper background.

It is no disgrace to have a poor academic background. But don't let that stop you from improving it and going on in your schooling.

POOR COLLEGE GRADES

You cannot change the past. You must live with those grades until you demonstrate a new record.

1. Determine why your grades were not good. Make specific corrections accordingly.
2. You may need to repeat a course or two for no credit, just to learn the material properly. If you received a C, D, or F in a basic course, that would be a reason to repeat it. Lay a good foundation before going on.
3. Consider carrying a lighter course load to allow

more concentration for higher grades which would offset
your low ones.

4. Review Chapters 5 and 6 to help you determine
   your personal ability and set realistic goals.
5. When you do get into academic trouble in the
   future, consider withdrawing from the course
   rather than adding another bad grade to your
   record.

Remember how difficult it was to raise a low GPA.
One full year with a C+ average (2.25) requires a full year
of A- work (3.75) to give you a B (3.00) average. Once you
get in grade trouble, it often takes the rest of your college
career to make it up.

DROPPING COURSES

One of the most common advising problems occurs when a
student wants to drop a course. In general, students should
select a course load and finish it. However, sometimes
situations occur when it is wise to drop a course.

- You do not have the necessary background to
  understand the material.
- You are overloaded academically and do not have
  the time to handle it.
- You need to concentrate on doing *very well* in
  fewer courses rather than risk another bad grade.

In dropping courses, observe a few practical cautions.

1. Talk with the professor before dropping a course.
   They generally want to help. You may not be in as
   much trouble as you suspect.
2. Don't necessarily drop the course in which you
   have the most difficulty. If it is part of a sequence
   of courses or a prerequisite course, be cautious.
   Perhaps you should drop a less important course

instead.

3. Don't get in the habit of dropping courses. Learn how to handle difficult ones.

Dropping a class is like an emergency crash landing in an airplane; do it if necessary for survival, but do it cautiously.

CHANGING MAJORS

What person at age eighteen knows precisely what he or she wishes to do for a lifetime? Very few. So why should changing majors be so bad? Like marriage, it's better to find out it won't work *before* the wedding.

Many factors cause a person to want to change majors: grades, experience in a particular field of study, changing goals, counsel, and many other inputs. Most students will change their major at least once, and their mind many more times.

You know your personal background, abilities and interests which narrow down the possibilities of a choice of major. But from that point, many choices still exist. Consider the following suggestions as guidelines:

1. As you enter your freshman year, attempt to decide between science or liberal arts courses.
2. By the end of the freshman year, enroll in a specific major, even if you are not quite sure it is the right direction. At least you are pointed towards a goal.
3. By the end of your sophomore year, settle on a specific major.
4. If you change majors later than your sophomore year, realize you may need to add a year to your undergraduate studies.
5. When you are one to one-and-a-half years away from a specific degree, complete it even if you

know you want a different major. After finishing that degree, you can do graduate study in the other field or simply complete the requirements for a second undergraduate degree. Many courses will overlap and count toward both degrees. Of course a change from engineering to history would not be compatible, but many switches to related fields would certainly work.

6. If you are tempted to change majors more than twice, sit back and reevaluate your whole direction in school. If you are that uncertain or undecided, perhaps you need to consider more basic issues relating to your life goals. If the changes result from doing poorly in a major, a review of your study habits and personal discipline is in order.

MONEY

The rising cost of an education makes money a key issue for students and parents. You must have it to go to school.

The basic sources of student financing are:

- personal funds
- parental support
- working while in school
- scholarships or grants
- loans

Regardless of where the support originates, it brings certain obligations. These obligations vary from maintaining a certain GPA to repaying some of the finances.

Obviously, we all would like the freedom to not have obligations attached to the money and still retain total control of its use. But that doesn't develop a sense of responsibility.

Most students' parents support them to some degree.

Thus, students have some responsibility to their parents. If conflict with parents ensues over finances, you may want to agree to treat their support as a loan, or perhaps earn your own way. This demonstrates your willingness to be personally responsible for your support and education.

Whenever possible, go to school full time with very little work. This gives maximum freedom for involvement in ministry and school. Many scholarships and grants are available when financial need is demonstrated.

The higher your grades and the greater your need, the easier it will be to get financial aid. When you obtain the money for school, use it wisely, and work hard to justify the investment.

Loans are the least desirable way to finance your education. They restrict you for several years to come while you pay back the loan. Yet, if your objective is to graduate, a loan may be worth it to avoid excessive work during the school term.

WORK

Many students must work to finance their way through college. Few finance themselves totally, but many do so partially.

For maximum use of school time for studies and ministry activity, it would be better not to work during the term.

Work puts a great deal of extra pressure on the student, and often leads to lower grades. My lowest grades occurred while I was working.

If work increases, your credit load may need to decrease. Usually, a student can handle 10 hours of work without reducing the credit load. Then for every 2½ to 3 hours of additional work time, 1 credit hour should be dropped. Thus, if a student works 20 hours, the credit load should be 3 to 4 hours less.

Some students burden themselves with a higher number of work hours and still keep a normal class load, thus eliminating any time for ministry or extracurricular activities. In so doing, they miss some of the greatest opportunities for spiritual development they will ever have. Sacrifice a few credit hours and extend college by a term to be involved in a campus ministry.

When one is involved in a campus ministry, another conflict with work frequently surfaces. Summer conferences and training experiences provide unique opportunities for specialized development. But they often conflict with work for part or all of the summer. This conflict provides a great opportunity to trust God to resolve it.

In some cases you can continue work and spiritual development at the same time during the summer. In any case, you will have opportunity for significant lordship decisions as you make your summer plans. Many parents see the development opportunities in such conferences and programs and will encourage and support you. Other parents will be opposed because of finances or their view of spiritual training. Whichever situation you encounter, you will find ample growth opportunities as you seek God's will and communicate it outwardly to your parents.

You can still be involved in a campus ministry when you must work. It will take hard work and discipline on your part, but you will also value the involvement more.

****

Many tasks worth doing do not come easily. Determination, work, and discipline provide the means for reaching a worthwhile goal. If that goal is your college education, then the principles in this book will give you significant help. But applying them is up to you.

> *The heights by great men reached and kept*
> *Were not attained by sudden flight,But they,*
> *While their companions slept,*
> *Were toiling upward in the night.*
>
> Henry Wadsworth Longfellow[3]

NOTES

1. As quoted in *Bits and Pieces*,(Fairfield, New Jersey: Economics Press; March, 1976), page 13.
2. As quoted in *The International Encyclopedia of Thoughts*, (Chicago: J.G. Ferguson Publishing Company, 1969), page 770.
3. Ibid., page 553.

Appendix A

The Arrow by Dan Greene

This arrow represents man plunging through time. Let's mark off a segment to indicate recorded history—that period of time for which we have some record of what has happened.

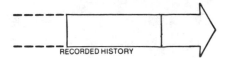

RECORDED HISTORY

It is striking to note that during man's entire history, his life has been characterized by STRIFE: international strife, local strife, personal strife. Even more striking is the fact that as of today, no particular solution has been found for this problem.

STRIFE

RECORDED HISTORY

If we assume that man is simply the product of his environment and that his basic tendencies toward strife represent a natural instinct for survival, then we are left with little hope for the future. When we review the constancy of strife throughout history, it appears that war and cruelty are here to stay. What is, is. It is as simple as that. Some cling doggedly to their faith in man's inevitable rise to reason and self-respect. But the history we are writing today—at man's most advanced state—is proving them wrong.

Because of this dilemma of man, the message of Jesus Christ becomes desperately crucial. Jesus explained that God did not create man for a life to be characterized by cruelty and strife, but by LOVE.

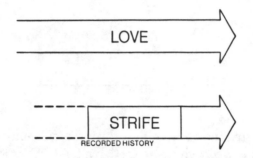

Jesus summed up God's plan for man in this simple way: Man was created to "'Love the Lord your God with all your heart and with all your soul and with all your strength and with all your mind'; and, 'Love your neighbor as yourself'" (Luke 10:27). Genuine love should be our controlling instinct toward God and toward each other.

Furthermore, Christ upheld and quoted the Old Testament record of human origin where we find that man is not simply the product of time and chance. He is not a meaningless bit of protoplasm that has evolved out of nothing. Rather, he is the creative work of an infinite God who gave man some of his personal characteristics.

He made man in his own image. Man could love, be truthful, just, selfless. Along with this, however, God also gave man the freedom of moral choice—the ability to remain in this God-like position or to step outside it and do the un-God-like thing. The biblical record indicates that man did exercise his free moral choice against God's directions. As a consequence, he fell into the life of strife.

That action of free moral choice against God is what the Bible calls SIN. "Therefore, just as sin entered the world through one man, and death through sin, and in this way death came to all men, because all sinned" (Romans 5:12). The distance I am from what God wants me to be is the measure of my sin.

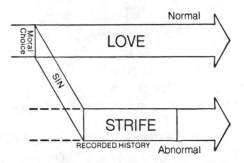

This is extremely significant, for it means that man is not designed for a life full of strife nor has he always been that way. It means that life as we know it today is not normal; it is abnormal. Normal life is that God-like life of love so well exemplified by Jesus Christ. If only God had provided a way back to him from this life of strife, then we could believe that a good God exists.

The resounding message of Scripture is just that: *God has provided a way back.* That way is Jesus. At a certain point in man's plunge through time, God interrupted human history by the entrance of his Son, Jesus Christ, who himself became the way back to the God-like life of love.

"For God so loved the world that he gave his one and only Son, that whoever believes in him shall not perish but have eternal life" (John 3:16).

"I came from God and now am here. I have not come

101

on my own; but he sent me" (John 8:42).

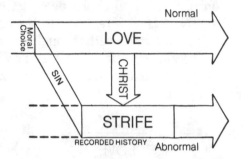

Jesus is not man's best efforts to find God. He is God's plan to reach man. John 14:6 says, "I am the way and the truth and the life. No one comes to the Father except through me."

How is Christ the way back? How did he do all this? He did it by going to the cross and there dealing with the real moral guilt that separated man from God. At the cross he erased that guilt and sin through his death for us. "For Christ died for sins once for all, the righteous for the unrighteous, to bring you to God" (1 Peter 3:18).

Now, with the problem of sin and guilt removed by Christ, any person can respond to Christ and be transferred back to the life of love and enjoy once again the originally intended relationship with God.

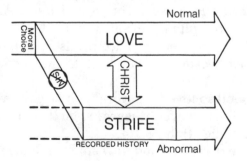

That personal response of the individual is all-important. You must acknowledge Jesus Christ as your Redeemer, as your personal Savior, and invite him to assume his rightful place in your life; to cleanse it, to change it, and to run it.

He, of course, has been waiting a long time to do just that. "Here I am! I stand at the door and knock. If anyone hears my voice and opens the door, I will go in and eat with him, and he with me" (Revelation 3:20).

There is a final note of warning. I don't say this as a threat and must explain that I find no personal pleasure in relating it. But it is nevertheless true and vitally important. "Just as man is destined to die once, and after that to face judgement, so Christ was sacrificed once to take away the sins of many people" (Hebrews 9:27-28).

I have only this life to cross from strife to love. Beyond the grave there is no crossing. In other words, my eternal destiny depends on my personal response to Christ now.

If I do nothing regarding Christ and remain on this world's present course, I will enter into ETERNAL SEPARATION FROM GOD; eternal strife. But if I cross the bridge now, I will enter into ETERNITY WITH HIM. That is heaven.

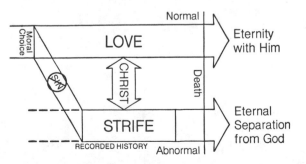

Annotated Bibliography

The following books may be helpful in special areas of need as you develop your study habits. They are all written from a secular viewpoint.

Adler, Mortimer J., and Van Doren, Charles. *How to Read a Book*. New York: Simon & Schuster, 1972. ($4.95)
A thorough text on reading and comprehending various types of books. Chapters of special interest are on how to read history, science, mathematics, philosophy, and social science. It is a classic, first published in 1940.

Bamman, Henry A., and Brammer, Lawrence M. *How to Study Successfully*. Palo Alto, California: Pacific Books, Publishers, 1959. ($1.25)
A brief study generally emphasizing the liberal arts preparation, writing, and vocabulary. It contains an interesting checklist of study habits for self-analysis.

Brechner, Irv. *The College Survival Kit*. New York: Bantam Books, 1975. ($2.95)
An interesting, brief summary of survival strategies for college. Each section is readable and succinct, but lacks much detail. It contains good sections on reading, notetaking, writing papers, and taking exams.

Crow, Lester and Alice. *How to Study*. New York: Collier Books, 1963. ($1.95)
This book presents a study method developed at Ohio State University. It combines several good self-

analysis checklists. It focuses on reading, notetaking, and memorizing.

Deese, James and Ellin K. *How to Study.* New York: McGraw-Hill, Inc., 1957, 1969, 1979. ($4.95)
This is a very good handbook. The first two chapters are helpful in self-analysis of your motivation and ability. The section on taking exams is helpful.

Gross, Michael J. *The How to Go to College Book.* Seattle, Washington: Passage Publishing, 1978. ($4.50)
This book contains an excellent section on taking examinations. It also has a short section on studying various types of courses and a longer section on writing term papers. It is an excellent resource.

Pauk, Walter. *How to Study in College.* Boston: Houghton Mifflin Company, 1962 and 1974. ($6.95)
This book contains general study methods plus several specialized sections, such as how to study mathematics, science, and foreign languages. It also has good sections on concentration and memory. The section on studying for and taking exams is worthwhile. It contains considerable material on notetaking and studying for liberal arts courses.

Other References of Interest

Brownstein, Samuel C., and Weiner, Mitchel. *Barron's How to Prepare for the Graduate Record Examination.* Woodbury, New York: Barron's Educational Series, Inc., 1973.

Cantor, Norman P. *How to Study History.* New York: Crowell, 1967.

Ehrlic, Eugene. *How to Study and Get Higher Grades.* New York: Crowell, 1961.

Ehrlic, Eugene, and Murphy, Daniel. *Writing and Researching Term Papers and Reports.* New York: Bantam Books, 1964.

Finkel, Lawrence S., and Krawlitz, Ruth. *How to Study and Improve Test-Taking Skills*, 2nd ed. New York: Oceana, Dobbs Ferry, 1976.

Hanau, Laia. *The Study Game.* New York: Harper & Row, 1974.

Hanau, Laia, and Niemeyer, Theo. *The Study Game Workbook.* New York: Harper & Row (LMR Books), 1976.

Millman, Jason, and Pauk, Walter. *How to Take Tests.* New York: McGraw-Hill, 1969.